June '03
Father's Day
From Andy

June '03
Father's Day

KANSAS CITY SOUTHERN In Color

by Jim Boyd

JIM BOYD

The Era of "Streamlined Hospitality"

1940 - 1970

Published by

Morning Sun Books, Inc.

9 Pheasant Lane
Scotch Plains, NJ 07076

Library of Congress
Catalog Card No. 2002112714

First Printing
ISBN 1-58248-107-5

Book design and layout by Jim Boyd

Visit us on the World Wide Web at:
www.morningsunbooks.com

Printed in Korea

𝒟edication

*IT IS DOUBTFUL that the KCS had any more loyal fans
than Tillie and Warren Caileff of Shreveport, Louisiana.
Both excellent photographers, they have been documenting
the KCS for longer than it would be polite to admit, and
they have been very generous in sharing their material with
numerous publishers. I met the Caileffs in 1968 through
our mutual friends Bill Sharp of Texarkana and Bill
McCaskill of Pine Bluff and was able to renew
old friendships via the Internet while working on this book.
Thank y'all for everything!*

TILLIE and WARREN CAILEFF with KCS-2 at Shreveport on November 14, 2002.

Acknowledgements

THE AUTHOR would like to thank the following people for their contributions to this book: Publisher Bob Yanosey gathered an impressive array of imagery, including the photos from Emery Gulash and Matt Herson. Special thanks go Warren and Tillie Caileff for their photos and help in refreshing my memories of the KCS, and to Bill and Betty Sharp for sharpening my recollections of their hometown of Texarkana and for their hospitality back in 1968 when I was a frequent visitor to their home. Also thanks to Jim Neubauer for his photo story on the ride to Noel, Mo., on the *Southern Belle*. Joe Van Hoorebeke made available his collection of builders plates, Marc Murtray and Kent Anderson helped with research, and Danny Johnson put me in touch with many of the other contributors.

This book would have been impossible without the contributions of the following photographers: Mike Abalos, Andover Junction Publications, Arthur Angstadt (Hawk Mountain Chapter NRHS), Don Ball, Jimmy Barlow, George Berisso, Roy F. Blackburn, A.E. Brown, Sandy Burton, Don Campbell, David Cash, the Conniff Railroadiana Collection, Bob Courtney, Bob Eisthen, R. Fillman, David Graeff, Carl Graves, Emery Gulash, Lawson Hill (Boston Chapter NRHS), Daniel E. Johnson, Tom Kline, Terry LaFrance, D.L. Leggett, Jim Marcus, Keel Middleton, Alan Miller, Mac Owen, Bill G. Sharp, Bob Snare, Andy Taylor, Harold K. Vollrath, Rich Wallace, Paul Walters and Charles Winters.

The primary reference for the roster data in this book was Lou Marre and Gregory Sommers' excellent *Kansas City Southern in the Deramus Era* (Withers Publishing, 1999) and the extensive KCS and L&A reference material that is in the old *Railroad* Magazine files, now owned by Carstens Publications.

TILLIE CAILEFF

**REPOWERED ERIE BUILT 60 and five B-units had freight 42
northbound through Shreveport, La., on September 21, 1963.**

FOREWORD

JIM BOYD

KANSAS CITY SOUTHERN E7 No.7 on Train 15-9 to at Kansas City Union Station in 1963 with the cafe-lounge-obs still in NYC stainless.

MY FIRST ENCOUNTER with the KCS was at Kansas City in 1963, and I was immediately struck by the image of that ultimate oxymoron in modern railroading, its "colorful black streamliners." Ever since that time, I've thought of the KCS in terms of passenger trains, even though none of its streamliners survived to see Amtrak in 1971.

I renewed my acquaintance with the KCS in the spring of 1968 when I was working as a Field Instructor for GM's Electro-Motive Division and was assigned to the Cotton Belt at Pine Bluff, Arkansas. My duties included riding new SP SD45s on their first runs down to Texarkana, Texas, where the Cotton Belt crossed the KCS and Texas & Pacific. Because of the freight traffic patterns on the Cotton Belt, I often spent evenings and mornings in Texarkana waiting for a return ride to Pine Bluff.

That was rough duty. Texarkana had a beautiful Union Station serving the KCS,

T&P and MoPac that was within easy walking distance of the Cotton Belt yard office.

Freights were sparse on the KCS, but it was still running two streamliners in each direction, and all four just happened to hit Texarkana during the hours I was usually there. The northbound *Southern Belle* came through at 8:45 a.m., while southbound 15-9, the nameless remnant of the old *Flying Crow,* arrived at 10:20 a.m. Northbound 10-16 arrived at 6:55 in the evening, followed an hour later by the southbound *Belle* at 8:00. Photo opportunities between March and July 1968 were incredible.

In the next few years I got to explore the KCS from Kansas City to New Orleans, as its freight power went from "blonde" F-units to white SD40s. While the KCS of today is a renegade survivor, I still think of it in terms of its glory days of the spring of 1968.

JIM BOYD

CRANDON LAKES, NEW JERSEY

SEPTEMBER 11, 2002

CONTENTS

FOREWORD / 3 INTRODUCTION / 5

CHAPTER 1
A Tale of Three Railroads : The KCS, LR&N and L&A / 6

CHAPTER 2
KCS Steam Power / 18 Steam on the L&A / 24

CHAPTER 3
Dieselizing the KCS/L&A / 28
Railroading During the War / 36 Diesels After the War / 39
The "New" *Southern Belle* of 1949 / 54
1052: The E8s Arrive / 60 Switchers and Geeps / 64
1953: A Few More Geeps / 68
New High-Hood Alcos in 1956? / 28 Birth of the Blondes / 72

CHAPTER 4
A New Generation / 74 "Second Generation" E7s / 78
New Passenger Cars in the 1960s / 82

CHAPTER 5
The Last Colorful Decade / 88 "Science Fiction" Cabooses / 97
Round Trip: Kansas City to Noel / 120

Chapter 6
The Future Looks Gray / 123

TEXARKANA UNION STATION was on the east-west Missouri Pacific and Texas & Pacific main line and required an eastward swing off the north-south KCS. The northbound *Southern Belle* (above) was backing around the wye off the KCS main in April 1968, with its E8 reflecting in the "black mirror" of the coach side. Southbound 15-9 (left) pulled directly into the station in March 1968.

INTRODUCTION

KANSAS CITY SOUTHERN was one of the first railroads to operate a "real" non-articulated diesel-powered streamliner when it introduced the *Southern Belle* in 1940. Over the next 30 years the image and spirit of "Streamlined Hospitality" defined the railroad.

The KCS and L&A were created, merged and operated by men with strong ideas and personalities. It was never a conformist, heading south when everyone else was scrambling westward and embracing the concept of long, slow freights when everyone else was focusing on high speed service. The route of the *Flying Crow* should have been a dead duck by the 1970s, but it made its way to the 21st Century as a major independent player in the merger game. Its most colorful era, however, were those three fascinating decades illustrated herein.

CHAPTER 1

IT WAS NOT THE BEST OF TIMES to start building a railroad, because in 1886 the Union Pacific transcontinental had been completed since 1869, and the Santa Fe was already into San Diego. But 27-year-old Kansas City insurance man Arthur Stilwell was looking to fulfill his childhood ambition of becoming a railroad magnate. His grandfather, Hamblin Stilwell, of Rochester, N.Y., had been one of the founders of the New York Central and a builder of the Erie Canal, as well as being a friend of Commodore Vanderbilt. Young Arthur had gotten into the insurance business in Connecticut and had moved west to exploit the opportunities in Kansas City, where he pioneered mortgage insurance and affordable home financing for working people.

But the prairie geography was irresistible for Stilwell, and his dream was to build a railroad due south from Kansas City to the Gulf of Mexico. In 1886 a former mayor of Kansas City, Edward L. Martin, told Stilwell of an option he was holding for the building of a railroad belt line through the industries and stockyards of the Missouri and Kaw river valleys. Stilwell offered to finance the project, and in 1890 it opened as the Kansas City Suburban Belt Railroad between Argentine, Kansas, and Independence, Missouri.

The belt line was an immediate success, and Stilwell and Martin struck out south toward Joplin, Mo., as the Kansas City, Nevada & Fort Smith Railroad to tap coalfields and zinc and lead mines. Within the next few years Stilwell and associates expanded southward by acquiring lumberman W.L. Whitaker's Texarkana & Fort

KCS PHOTO

ARTHUR STILWELL

Smith and Indian chief Mathias Splitlog's Kansas City, Fort Smith & Southern.

The Panic of 1893 threatened to dry up investment capital, but Stilwell traveled to Holland to drum up financing to expand his railroad, now called the Kansas City, Pittsburg & Gulf. His most enthusiastic backer was coffee merchant John DeGeoijen, whom he had befriended on a trans-Atlantic voyage a few years before. With DeGeoijen's help, Stilwell raised $3 million to finance the KCP&G's expansion, which amounted to fully one-third of America's total railroad construction for the panic year of 1893!

As a result of the Dutch investment, many of the towns created during the KCP&G's expansion were given Dutch names. "DeQueen," Ark., was as close as Stilwell could get to an American version of DeGeoijen, but Mena, Ark., was named for John DeGeoijen's wife Wilhelmina. In addition to Amsterdam, Mo., the Dutch names included Vandervoort, Ark.; Bloomberg and Nederland, Texas, and Zwolle, Hornbeck, DeRidder and DeQuincy, La.

Stilwell continued building south through Texarkana to Shreveport. He almost bought the Houston, East & West Texas to get into Galveston, but he had a strange fear of what could happen to that Gulf city's unprotected harbor in case of a severe hurricane. Stilwell declined to purchase the Galveston line and pursued his original plan to build due south to a spot on the inland Lake Sabine and to dig a ship canal from that secure harbor to the Gulf. The terminal city was to be named Port Arthur in his honor. The decision to go to Port

A TALE OF THREE RAILROADS:

PORT ARTHUR, TEXAS, named for Arthur Stilwell, was the Gulf terminal for the KCP&G. Shortly after 1900, KCS 4-4-0 106 had a small train at the imposing station there.

Arthur turned out to be a good one, because only four years after the KCP&G passed up the option to get into Galveston, that city's harbor was devastated by a hurricane in September 1900.

Through service was inaugurated between Kansas City and Port Arthur on the KCP&G on September 11, 1897, and prairie grain began moving through the portside elevators, and the railroad was doing a fine business hauling coal, lumber and agricultural products.

A strange fate befell Arthur Stilwell just after the KCP&G was completed. He needed rolling stock for his soon-to-be-thriving but cash-strapped railroad and went to his old friend George M. Pullman to finance it. George M. agreed on a handshake to a $3 million loan, and 1000 boxcars cars were immediately ordered with long-term financing. In the week or so that it took Stilwell to draw up the proper legal papers and get to Chicago on October 19, 1897, for Pullman's signature on the deal, the

pioneer sleeping car builder died! The KCP&G was suddenly $3 million in debt and ultimately driven into bankruptcy. Stilwell was forced out by the new Board of Directors. Arthur Stilwell was much better at building railroads than running them, and he spent the rest of his life promoting the Kansas City, Mexico & Orient but died in an elevator accident in New York in 1928 before seeing it completed. (Do not confuse Arthur Stilwell with Lewis Buckley Stillwell, who designed the unusual "Stillwell" passenger cars in 1912 for the Pressed Steel Car Co. that were made famous by the Erie.)

The Kansas City, Pittsburg & Gulf was reorganized as the Kansas City Southern in 1900 with the highly respected Col. Samuel Fordyce as its president. Fordyce had been a powerful influence on the railroads of the region and was credited with the successful emergence of the Cotton Belt from a series of bankruptcies. Col. Fordyce guided the KCS for only the year of 1900 and was succeeded in that post by Stuart Knott in 1901 and Job Adolphus Edson in 1905.

The KCS, LR&N AND L&A

Stilwell's decision to build his own railroad into Beaumont and Port Arthur instead of buying the line to Galveston proved to be a remarkable stroke of luck for the new KCS,

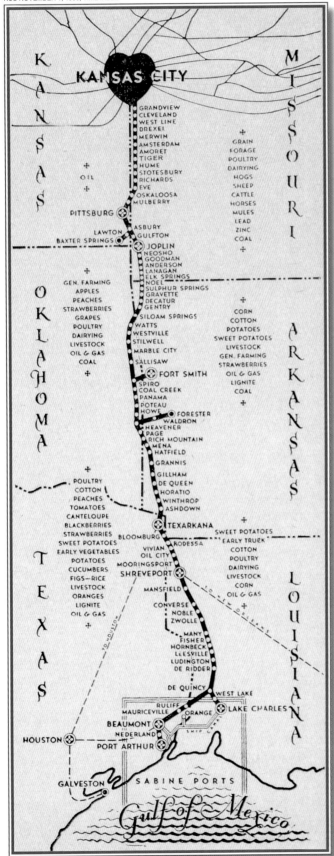

because in 1901 a huge plume of crude oil erupted from Lucas No.1, and America had its first "gusher" oil well. The Spindletop oil field was right under the KCS! The entire area from Port Arthur to Beaumont and Lake Charles quickly sprouted refineries and became one of the world's greatest producers of petroleum products.

The KCS soon emerged into the 20th Century as a prosperous and well-managed company that fulfilled its destiny going straight "as the crow flies" from Kansas City to the Gulf of Mexico. Of course, that particular crow got a bit erratic when it encountered the Ozarks, Ouachitas and Rich Mountain.

Louisiana Railway & Navigation

About the time the KCP&G was anchoring itself in Port Arthur, in July 1897 St. Louis entrepreneur William Edenborn saw the economic potential in building a railroad from Shreveport to New Orleans and began constructing his Shreveport & Red River Valley toward Baton Rouge. And it was literally "his" railroad. William Edenborn had been born in Prussia in 1848 and emigrated to the U.S. in 1867 at the age of 19, following a technical school education and working experience with the Krupp steel works. He settled in St. Louis and continued his pursuit of the steel business. After inventing a process for mass producing

INDIAN CHIEF Mathias Splitlog owned Kansas City, Ft. Smith & Southern, which had this splendid parlor car *Bird-in-Hand*. Texarkana & Fort Smith 4-4-0 No.5 had a work train on the Arkansas River bridge (right) at Redland, Okla., prior to creation of KCS in 1900.

JIM BOYD

wire nails, he built a career that ultimately won him a seat on the Board of Directors of U.S. Steel. The Shreveport-New Orleans railroad was one of the investments made possible by his rapidly growing personal fortune.

THE LOUISIANA RAILWAY & NAVIGATION COMPANY began service into New Orleans in 1906. This trestle over the Bonnet Carre Floodway was built in the mid-1930s to help resist Mississippi River flooding. An eastbound freight was headed up by F9Am 90 (originally F7 73D) in August 1969.

The Shreveport & Red River Valley bridged the Red River at Alexandria in 1902 and began reaching across the swamplands toward the Mississippi River on a roadbed of submerged cypress logs buried in iron ore. The Mississippi itself would be crossed with a stern-wheeler ferryboat and barge between Naples and Angola, 50 miles upriver from Baton Rouge. In May 1903 the S&RRV was renamed The Louisiana Railway & Navigation Company. Freight service between Shreveport and New Orleans was inaugurated on December 12, 1906.

Edenborn paid for the construction of the LR&N with his own money and took a personal interest in developing online business and maintaining a first-class operation. In 1923 he acquired a Katy branch and some Texas & Pacific trackage rights to lace together a line

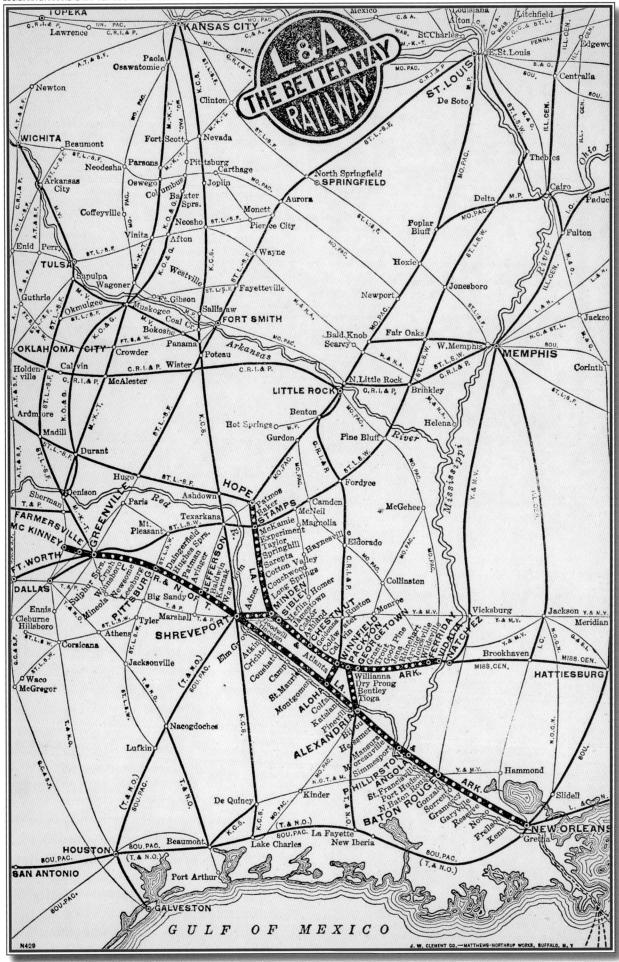

reaching into Greenville and Dallas, Texas. As required by Texas state law, the line was incorporated in the Lone Star State as Louisiana Railway & Navigation Company of Texas. Edenborn ran the system as his personal empire until his death on May 14, 1926.

Louisiana & Arkansas

During 1896, the same year that William Edenborn was building his S&RRV east from Shreveport, lumber man William Buchanan had built a huge sawmill alongside the Cotton Belt at Stamps, Ark., and began constructing a railroad south to tap his timber stands. Because it would cross a state line, his Louisiana & Arkansas Railway was chartered as a common carrier, and by June 1902 it had grown 115 miles south to Winnfield, Louisiana.

To gain additional northern rail connections,

HOPE, ARKANSAS, was the northern end of the Louisiana & Arkansas and its connection with the MoPac main line and a Frisco branch. Freshly painted L&A F3 95 was at Hope in April 1968 (above). All of the 1948 14-roomette, 4-double-bedroom sleepers were owned by the L&A and named for system presidents. The *Harvey Couch* (below) was on the *Southern Belle* No.2 at Texarkana in 1968.

Buchanan extended the L&A 23 miles up from the mill at Stamps to the Missouri Pacific main line and a Frisco branch at Hope, Ark. By this time, Minden, La., had become the headquarters and focal point of the L&A, and

TWO PHOTOS / JIM BOYD

in 1910 railroad was extended 30 miles west from Minden to get into Shreveport.

Over the next few years the L&A built southward from Winnfield to Pacton, where the line split, with one leg going south to Alexandria to connect with Edenborn's LR&N and the other striking east through Jena to Vidalia, where it could use the Missouri Pacific's carferry to cross the Mississippi River to Natchez. The L&A by 1911 was a booming railroad benefitting from the oil patch prosperity of the region.

Like the Louisiana Railway & Navigation Company, the L&A was essentially owned by one man, William Buchanan, and when he died on October 26, 1923, his widow had little interest in running a railroad and was quite willing to sell it.

Harvey Couch and the L&A

Harvey Crowley Couch was an electric power company executive who had once worked as a Railway Post Office clerk and was still fascinated by railroads. He recognized the L&A as an excellent property and saw William Buchannan's heirs' disinterest in the railroad as a business opportunity. He negotiated a purchase of the L&A and took over as its owner and president in early 1928.

The same opportunity was immediately presented him by the death two years earlier of William Edenborn and his widow's eagerness to sell that railroad. Couch purchased the Louisiana Ry. & Navigation Co. and merged it into the L&A on May 1, 1928. Because they had both been privately owned and financed, both the L&A and LR&N were prosperous and debt-free as they entered the Great Depression while still benefitting from the oil boom.

Harvey Couch saw the logic of a merger between the KCS and his expanded L&A. The L&A was stronger than the

HARVEY C. COUCH

KCS, and his first move was to attempt to have the L&A buy the KCS, but the Interstate Commerce Commission rejected this approach. Undaunted, he began to purchase stock in the KCS and soon gained a seat on the Board of Directors. He became Board Chairman on May 27, 1937, and began to align both of his properties into a "merger" that would satisfy the ICC. On October 20, 1939, the ICC approved the KCS acquiring stock control of the L&A, although both railroads would maintain their legal and financial identities. While they were consolidated under the Kansas City Southern image, equipment was still purchased and lettered for the individual companies and would remain that way until 1992! Although Kansas City Southern was the "surviving" company, in reality it was Harvey Couch and the L&A that had taken over the historic KCS.

The new combined KCS/L&A was placed under the presidency of Harvey's younger brother, Charles "Peter" Couch, in October 1939 when Harvey left the railroad to become a director of President Roosevelt's Reconstruction Finance Corporation.

The Deramus Dynasty

On November 9. 1909, a 21-year-old Southern Railway dispatcher from Memphis went to work for the KCS and began a family dynasty that would last until 1990. William Neal Deramus had been born in Coopers, Ala., in 1888 and began tending switch lamps and learning the telegraph at the L&N depot there at age 13. Within two years he was the relief operator. He went on to the Atlantic Coast Line and became a dispatcher for the Southern at Memphis by age 20. When his Memphis chief dispatcher moved to the KCS, he invited his eager new dispatcher to join him in Pittsburg, Kansas.

WILLIAM NEAL DERAMUS

Deramus advanced rapidly from dispatcher to Southern Division superintendent in 1925. When Harvey Couch took over the KCS in May 1939 and combined it with the L&A on October 20, Bill Deramus was effectively "running the railroad" as vice president and general manager. The system had by then survived the Depression and grown to its "modern" size, bought massive Lima 2-10-4s and introduced its first diesel-powered streamliner.

With the merger, the ailing Harvey Couch immediately handed the presidency of the newly combined railroad to his younger brother Peter. Shortly after Harvey died in 1940, Peter resigned to handle the family's numerous other business interests. In August 1941 he placed the company's presidency in the hands of his trusted operating man, Executive Vice President William N. Deramus.

A.E. BROWN

THE *FLYING CROW*, No.15, was striding southward (above) at Forbing, La., just south of Shreveport, on October 13. 1946, behind bald-faced 4-6-2 801. Typical power for L&A's *Shreveporter* and *Hustler* was one of the three ex-LR&N Baldwin 4-6-0s, 392-394. The 393 (below) was at Bossier City, La., in April 1938.

HAROLD K. VOLLRATH COLLECTION

Passenger Service

On the verge of the merge of the KCS and L&A in 1939, the two railroads were running a credible if minimal post-Depression passenger service. The KCS covered its Kansas City to Port Arthur main line with a single train in each direction, Nos. 15 and 16, the *Flying Crow*. Its historic name was derived from the road's slogan "Straight As The Crow Flies" from Kansas City to the Gulf.

The *Crow* was a leisurely heavyweight that made all the stops and took about 26 hours to make its 788.6-mile journey, but it carried a 12-section Drawing Room sleeper and a diner, as well as a U.S. mail contract. It was a night train on the north end, departing Kansas City at 10:00 p.m. southbound and arriving at 8:10 a.m. northbound. It was a day

KCS PUBLIC TIMETABLE / NOVEMBER 1, 1936

KANSAS CITY SOUTHERN
≶ STRAIGHT AS THE CROW FLIES ≷

Equipment

TRAIN 15—"THE FLYING CROW"
12-Section Drawing Room Sleeper—Kansas City to Port Arthur.
Coaches and Chair Cars.
Dining Cars serving all meals.

TRAIN 16—"THE FLYING CROW"
12-Section Drawing Room Sleeper — Port Arthur to Kansas City.
Coaches and Chair Cars.
Dining Cars serving all meals.

CONDENSED SCHEDULES

Tr. 15				Tr. 16
10 00	Lv.	Kansas City	Ar.	8 10
1 55	Ar.	Pittsburg	Lv.	4 30
2 50	Ar.	Joplin	Lv.	3 40
9 00	Ar.	Ft. Smith	Lv.	9 20
7 00	Lv.	Ft. Smith	Ar.	11 25
8 36	Lv.	Howe	Lv.	9 50
1 55	Ar.	Texarkana	Lv.	4 15
2 10	Lv.	Texarkana	Ar.	4 05
4 30	Ar.	Shreveport	Lv.	1 55
4 45	Lv.	Shreveport	Ar.	1 45
10 55	Ar.	Lake Charles	Lv.	7 45
11 25	Ar.	Beaumont	Lv.	7 25
12 15	Ar.	Port Arthur	Lv.	6 45

train in both directions south of Rich Mountain, although No.15 didn't finally make Port Arthur until after midnight. The *Flying Crow* had branch line connections to Fort Smith, Ark., and Lake Charles, Louisiana.

Power for the heavyweight *Crow* was generally a modest-sized 800-series 4-6-2 with 75-inch drivers. A few carried the *Flying Crow* herald on their tenders and embarrassed themselves with an air horn that made a "cawing" bird call.

The L&A covered its system with a train each way a day, though its route and service was a bit more complex than the KCS. L&A Trains 1 and 2, the *Shreveporter*, were effectively commuter trains over the 108 miles between Hope and Shreveport, although they carried sleepers to and from St. Louis connecting with MoPac's *Sunshine Special* southbound and *Texan* northbound. In 1930 L&A No.1 departed Hope at 6:05 in the morning and arrived at Shreveport's Central Station at 8:59. Following the business day, No.2 left Shreveport at 6:30 in the evening and got back to Hope at 8:25. A "doodlebug" motor car provided a daytime connection with Nos.1 and 2 between Minden and Winnfield with two J.G. Brill cars. The 125 was a 43-foot 1928 gas-mechanical, while the 126 was a bigger 73-foot 1929 gas-electric.

The 332-mile run between Shreveport and New Orleans via Minden was covered by the overnight *Hustler* (Nos. 204 and 203 between Shreveport and Minden and Nos. 3 and 4 from Minden to New Orleans.

While the *Hustler* carried a sleeper, its eleven-hour overnight schedule did not require a diner. Typical power was a former LR&N 390-series Baldwin 4-6-0.

The line to Greenville, Texas, out of Shreveport and the "Short Line" to Alexandria, La.,

were served by daily mixed trains in each direction. A mixed also covered the Winnfield to Vidalia line.

A Bridge and a Streamliner

The merger with the L&A in 1939 gave the KCS and entirely new marketing map. Instead of the relative "nowhere" that was Port Arthur, its southern terminal was now New Orleans – and there was no direct passenger service between Kansas City and New Orleans. By 1939 the idea of the diesel-powered streamliner was dazzling the public with the exploits of the Burlington's *Zephyr*

JOINING THE KCS AND L&A created a new route between Kansas City and New Orleans, and Harvey Couch wanted to capitalize on it by introducing a brand new streamliner, the *Southern Belle*. Electro-Motive delivered two E3 diesels in July 1939 and a third (above) in June 1940, but the train could not be inaugurated until the passenger cars were delivered by Pullman and the bridge over the Mississippi River at Baton Rouge (below, in 1957) was completed in May 1940.

WHEN THE *SOUTHERN BELLE* was introduced in 1940, the KCS/L&A had three E3s. The 1-3 were renumbered 21-23 in 1942, and following World War II the nose herald was updated, and the dark green was changed to black (above). The 1, former EMC demonstrator 822, was at Kansas City (below) in 1940 in the lightning stripe *Flying Crow* livery.

and the Santa Fe's *Super Chief*, and the timing was perfect for the KCS to enter New Orleans in a dramatic new way.

Harvey Couch was willing to put up nearly a million Depression-era dollars to get the KCS into the streamliner business. Again, his timing was fortunate, because the idea of the articulated trainset like the Burlington's *Zephyr* and the GM&N's *Rebel* (that had been running into New Orleans since 1935) had been proven impractical, and the Electro-Motive Corporation (soon to be a division of General Motors) was introducing its first "standard" passenger diesel, the E3, using its new 567 diesel engine.

The KCS ordered three four-car trainsets from Pullman and two EMC 2000-h.p. E3 diesels. The Pullman-built cars were constructed of riveted aluminum alloy and consisted of

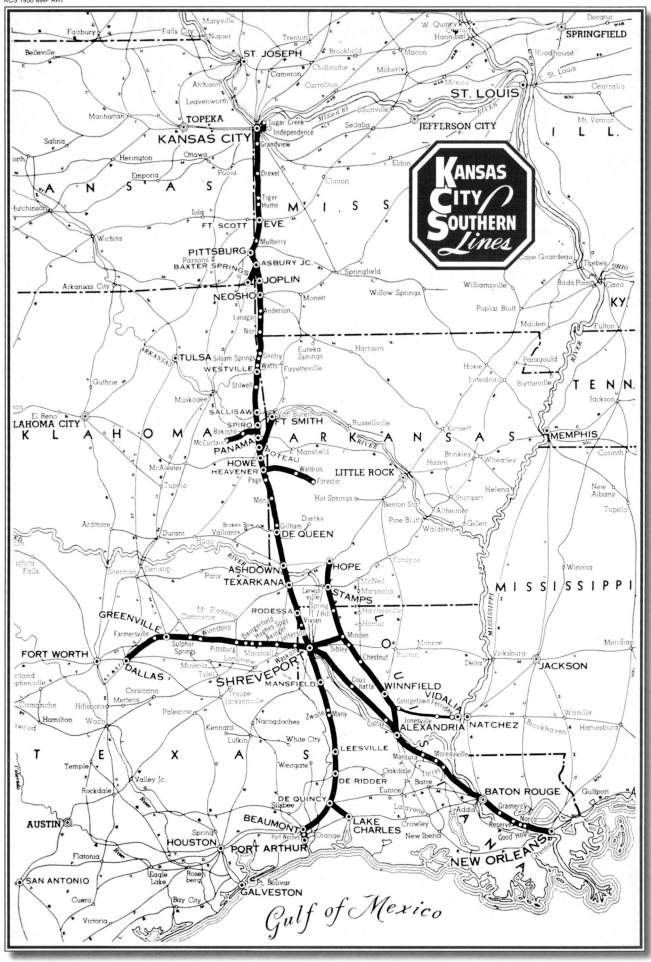

mail-baggage-express cars, coaches and three tavern-observations (*Good Cheer, Hospitality* and *Prairie Home*). Pullman assigned heavyweight sleepers but did its best to match the livery and disguise them as lightweight cars.

The new train was to be named the *Southern Belle*, and it was announced with a flurry of publicity, including a systemwide "Miss Southern Belle" contest to choose the young lady whose image would represent the train. The winner was Margaret Landry of Baton Rouge, and photos of her decked out in ante-bellum finery became the advertising theme for the streamliner.

The KCS purchased EMC's E3 demonstrator 822 (renumbering it KCS 1) and worked with the General Motors Styling Section in Detroit to develop the stunning dark green livery with red and yellow trim and silver roofs. Although the Pullman-oriented story in the October 5, 1940, *Railway Age* credits Pullman stylists with the exterior livery, the design much more closely reflects the GM Detroit stylists' characteristics.

The E3s 1 and 2 were delivered in a red and black lightning-stripe livery (**page 15**) on July 31, 1939, and put into service on the *Flying Crow* until the *Southern Belle* passenger cars could be delivered by Pullman. The E3s were sent back to EMC at La Grange in June 1940 and repainted into a new *Southern Belle* livery that placed more emphasis on the yellow. They were returned with a third E3 (**page 14**).

The Pullman trainsets were delivered, but the introduction of the *Southern Belle* was delayed by a few months until the new rail-highway bridge that the State of Louisiana was building over the Mississippi River at Baton Rouge was completed in May 1940 (**page 14**). This permitted the KCS to abandon the time-consuming ferry operation between Filston Landing and Angola that had replaced the original LR&N ferry at Naples in 1928. Had the Baton Rouge bridge not been built, just picture the elegant E3s waiting on either side while their streamliner was barged across the river by a stern-wheel steamboat.

The *Southern Belle* was put into service on September 1, 1940, and the KCS/L&A began a new era of "Streamlined Hospitality." ◙

WHEN BILL DERAMUS assumed the presidency of the KCS/L&A in the prewar calm of August 1941, he inherited a system that rostered one diesel switcher, three E-units and a strange mix of old and new steam power. Since no part of the KCS family dated further back than 1890, its earliest locomotives were relatively modern 4-4-0s, 2-6-0s and 4-6-0s.

A.E. BROWN

THE *FLYING CROW* was usually assigned an 800-series 4-6-2 (page 15), but on October 27, 1946, D-7 Ten-Wheeler 602 had No.15 rolling grandly through Forbing, Louisiana.

KCS motive power policy in the early 20th Century had developed under the influence of one of the more unlikely figures in American railroading. Leonor F. Loree represented the Eastern financial interests that controlled the KCS and was named chairman of its board of directors in 1906. The next year he also became chairman of the Delaware & Hudson. Loree had strong ideas about motive power and pressed his philosophies on the management of both the KCS and the D&H. He believed in tractive effort and as much weight as possible on the drivers, and both of his railroads were soon depending on ponderous 2-8-0s for freight power.

He had been president of the Baltimore & Ohio in 1904 when that railroad put into service America's first compound articulated, the 0-6-6-0 "Old Maud." In 1912 the KCS bought a dozen of the powerful, waddling monsters that it put to work, not as helpers as on the B&O, but as road power over Rich Mountain.

Class G 0-6-6-0s 700-711 were powerful, with 80,463 pounds of Tractive Effort (nearly

KCS Steam Power

18

CHAPTER 2

ROY F. BLACKBURN

SCHENECTADY BUILT SEVEN Class G-1 compound 2-8-8-0s (750-756) in 1918 and ten Class G-2 (757-766) in 1924. The 750 (above) was at Pittsburg, Kan., on May 4, 1936. Class E-3 Consolidation 480 (left) was typical of the KSC's largest group of 47 2-8-0s (475-499, 510-532) built between 1898 and 1907. The KCS used its dozen compound 0-6-6-0s (700-711) as road power. The 704 (bottom) was at Pittsburg in 1933. Note slide valves on the low pressure cylinders of both Mallets.

twice that of a 2-8-0), and hid their lack of a pilot truck behind an impressive cowcatcher. In 1918 the KCS followed up with seven huge compound Class G-1 2-8-8-0s (750-756) that had much better tracking characteristics than the 0-6-6-0s. In 1924 the KCS added ten more 2-8-8-0s, Class G-2 757-766, that produced 122,000 pounds of T.E. Not surprisingly, under Loree the D&H indulged in similar compounds of various wheel arrangements.

The KCS passenger power of that era was mostly 4-6-0s south of Shreveport and eleven lanky 75-inch-drivered 4-6-2s built by Alco in 1912 (Class H 800-807) and 1919 (Class H-1 808-810). Loree favored high boiler pressure, bald smokeboxes, high headlights and green-painted boiler jackets.

To serve customers in the Kansas City area that had some very steep grades on their industrial spurs, the KCS bought two huge three-truck Shays. The 900, built in 1913, had the biggest wheels (48-inch) and cylinders

WARREN CAILEFF COLLECTION

THREE-TRUCK SHAY 900 was purchased from Lima in 1913 to work steep industrial sidings in the Kansas City terminal area. The 130-ton 900 had the biggest drivers and cylinders ever applied to a Shay. Western Maryland 162-ton "Big 6," built in 1945 as Lima's last and heaviest Shay, was on the Cass Scenic Railroad (left) in May 1983. Although the 6 is superheated, the bigger cylinders gave saturated KCS 900 more Tractive Effort, 72,000 to 60,000 pounds.

Kansas City Southern Steam Locomotives 1891-1954

Type	Class	Numbers	Built	Driv.	Cyl.	B/P	T.E	Notes
2-4-4T	None	KCIAL 101-103	BLW 1892	56"	15x22	??	12,488	K.C. & Independence Air Line, not lettered KCS
2-4-4T	A	56	BLW 1893	52"	10&17x24	160	14,201	Ex-Union Terminal 56, sold 1918
4-4-0	B	T&FS 5	BLW 1893	63"	17x24	155	13,100	Texarkana & Ft. Smith; scrapped 1910
4-4-0	B	130-131	BLW 1892	63"	17x24	160	13,301	Ex-KCP&G 111-112, scrapped 1910-11
4-4-0	B-1	101-110	BLW 1895-97	63"	17x24	160	16,377	Ex-KCP&G, scrapped 1910-15
4-4-0	B-2	132	Alco/Brooks 1889	63"	17x24	160	13,301	Ex-KCFS&S 2, scrapped 1910
4-4-0	B-3	140-143	Alco/Sch. 1893-95	60"	18x24	160	17,626	Ex-KCP&G, disposed 1907-39
4-4-0	B-4	170-173	Manchester 1897	69"	18x24	180	17,242	Ex-KCP&G, scrapped 1923
4-4-0	None	AW 2	?? 1906	63"	17x24	??	13,000	Arkansas Western Ry.; sold 1908
2-6-0	C	240-241	BLW 1892	55"	18x24	160	17,401	Ex-KCP&G, nee-KCN&FS, disposed 1911
2-6-0	C-1	300-305	BLW 1895	55"	19x24	165	22,763	Ex-KCP&G 21-26, scrapped 1911-13
2-6-0	C-1	65	BLW 1899	51"	19x24	175	25,270	Rebuilt from F-1 0-6-0 65 in 1917; sold 1925
2-6-0	C-2	85	BLW 1907	51"	19x26	180	28,158	Rebuilt from F-2 0-6-0 85 in 1932; scrapped 1938
4-6-0	D	250-257	Manchester 1897	63"	18x24	160	17,835	Ex-KCP&G 40-47, disposed 1911-14
4-6-0	D-1	270-273	BLW 1893	55"	18x24	180	18,026	Ex-KCP&G 51-54, scrapped 1911-12
4-6-0	D-2	274	Alco/Brooks 1889	57"	18x24	160	17,394	Ex-KCFS&S 3, scrapped 1911
4-6-0	D-3	320-333	BLW 1896-97	55"	19x24	170	22,763	Ex-KCP&G 56-69, disposed 1907-24
4-6-0	D-4	334-337	Alco/Sch. 1893	55"	19x24	170	22,763	Ex-C&A 235-238, to KCS 1905, scrapped 1919
4-6-0	D-5	350-380	Baldwin 1898	55"	20x26	180	29,338	Ex-KCP&G 350-380, disposed 1916-40
4-6-0	D-6	400-411	Grant. 1897	63"	19x24	170	19,872	Ex-KCP&G 400-411, disposed 1910-27
4-6-0	D-7	600-606	BLW 1903	67"	20x26	200	26,389	Ex-500-506, rebuilt & re# 1908, disposed 1939-48
2-8-0	None	AW 1	Taunton 1893	51"	20x24	140	22,400	Arkansas Western Ry.; scrapped 1912
2-8-0	E-1	460-474	BLW 1900-03	57"	15&26x30	200	39,460	Vauclain Compound 420-434, simpled 1904-06
2-8-0	E-2	450-453	BLW 1903	51"	22x28	190	41,785	Built Pitts., Shawmut & Northern 50-53, sold 1917
2-8-0	E-3	475-499, 510-532	Alco & BLW 1906-08	55"	22x30	210	47,124	Some rebuilt as 1020-1031, disposed 1939-54
2-8-0	E-4	550-564	Alco/Richmond 1913	63"	26x30	200	55,948	Built with 57" drivers, 556, 559-560 not rebuilt.
0-6-0	F	51-55, 57-58	BLW 1891-95	51"	18x24	155	20.736	Ex-K.C. Suburban Belt and Union Terminal
0-6-0	F-1	59-66	BLW 1897-99	51"	19x24	165	23,826	Ex-KCSB 59-66 (TFS&W 59) Disposed 1917-25
0-6-0	F-2	81-100	BLW-1901-08	51"	19x26	180	28,158	Disposed 1929-1950
0-6-0	F-3	70-73	Alco/Sch. 1913	50"	20x28	180	34,300	Scrapped 1948-49
0-6-6-0	G	700-711	Alco/Sch. 1912	57"	22&35x32	220	80,463	All scrapped 1937 except 706 & 711 in 1947
2-8-8-0	G-1	750-756	Alco/Sch. 1918	57"	26&41x32	205	103,000	Scrapped 1939-49
2-8-8-0	G-2	757-766	Alco/Sch. 1924	57"	26&41x32	225	122,000	Scrapped 1947-53
2-8-8-0	G-2	758, 759, 762, 764	Alco/Sch. 1924	57"	26x32 (4)	250	125,000	Rebuilt as simple 1939-1942; scrapped 1952-53
4-6-2	H	800-807	Alco/Sch. 1912	75"	24x28	225	41,126	Scrapped 1951-54; 800 & 806 to L&A in 1939
4-6-2	H-1	808-810	Alco/Sch. 1919	75"	24x28	225	41,126	Scrapped 1951-53
2-10-4	J	900-909	Lima 1937	70"	27X34	310	93,300	900-904 oil, 905-909 coal; scrapped 1952-53
0-8-0	K	1000-1012	KCS 1924-29	55"	21x30	210	42,937	Rebuilt E-1 2-8-0s 460-/-474; scrapped 1948-53
0-8-0	K-1	1020-1031	KCS 1924-29	55"	22x30	210	47,124	Rebuilt E-3 2-8-0s 476-/-530; scrapped 1951-54
2-10-2	L	200-205	Alco/Brooks 1917	64"	27x32	210	75,059	Ex-Wabash, to KCS 1942, scrapped 1951-53
2-10-2	L-1	220-223	BLW 1919	57"	27x32	200	68,375	Ex-Ann Arbor, to KCS 1942, scrapped 1951-52
Shay	S	900	Lima 1913	48"	18x20 (3)	200	74,440	Three-truck Shay; scrapped 1929
Shay	S-1	901	Lima 1914	46"	17x18 (3)	200	62,500	Three-truck Shay; scrapped 1929

Roster compiled by Harold K. Vollrath in 1956 from KCS sources. for *Railroad* Magazine

THE KCS PITTSBURG SHOP rebuilt 25 Class E-1 and E-3 2-8-0s into 0-8-0 switchers in the late 1920s. One of the last KCS steam locomotives in service was 1005, at Kansas City on January 9, 1954 (below right) and on a transfer (above) on February 13, 1954. Class K 1005 was rebuilt from E-1 469 and scrapped at Pittsburg in March 1954. Consolidation 510, in an unidentified photo (below left), is typical of the E-3s that were rebuilt into the twelve Class K-1 0-8-0s 1020-1031.

WARREN CAILEFF COLLECTION

ABOVE and TOP / DON BALL COLLECTION

(18x20-inch) ever applied to a Shay. Lima's last Shay, Western Maryland 6, built in 1945, had the same wheels but slightly smaller cylinders, giving KCS 900 the edge in Tractive Effort (72,000 to 60,000 pounds), though the "Big 6" outweighed the 900 (324,000 pounds to 280,000 pounds). In 1914 the KCS bought an example of Lima's largest standard catalog model, the slightly smaller (260,000 pounds) three-truck 901.

Not surprisingly for a terminal railroad, the KCS also rostered a substantial fleet of 0-6-0 and 0-8-0 switchers. The 0-6-0s were built new between 1891 and 1913, but the 25 0-8-0s were all created in the Pittsburg Shops between 1924 and 1929 from Class E-1 and E-3 2-8-0s.

About this same time, Leonor Loree's son, James Tabor Loree, designed an auxiliary

booster engine for use in place of a tender truck that would add about 13,000 to 18,000 pounds of Tractive Effort to any locomotive. These "Bethlehem Auxiliary Locomotives" were applied to 0-6-0s, 0-8-0s, 2-8-0s and some of the 2-8-8-0 Mallets and saw extensive use on Loree's Delaware & Hudson, as well.

Another experiment was the use of pulverized coal in two of the 2-8-8-0s. Stationary power plants are almost universally fired with clean burning pulverized coal, and two huge new tenders were built with pulverizing machinery for grinding up the coal before feeding it into the firebox. In 1925 the 766 was tested on pulverized coal, and in 1929 the 750 was fitted with an improved version of the equipment. By 1930 both were restored to oil burners. The two huge tenders were stripped of their

THE STANDARD PASSENGER ENGINES on the pre-L&A merger KCS were eight Class H (800-807) and three Class H-1 4-6-2s (808-810) built by Alco/Schenectady in 1912 and 1919. The 806 was photographed (above) in Kansas City before being transferred to the L&A in 1940. The 803 (below) was equipped with one of the huge tenders that were built for the pulverized coal experiments on two 2-8-8-0s in the 1920s. Note the silver smokebox door and cylinder heads. In the 1940s the specially decorated 803 was kept at Pittsburg so that if the *Southern Belle* was running late the Pacific could be used to forward the passenger train into Kansas City and back so that the single diesel unit could be serviced at Pittsburg instead of during the turn-around at K.C. With the big tender, it needed no water stops.

pulverizers and went into service behind a variety of locomotives, the most bizarre of which was 4-6-2 803, that was almost dwarfed by the tender itself!

The KCS struggled through the Depression with its WWI-era steam fleet. Bill Deramus was general manager when the KCS realized it needed more modern freight power, and its first move in that direction was to rebuild a dozen of the 57-inch-drivered E-4 2-8-0s with cast underframes and 63-inch Boxpok drivers.

But 2-8-0s were still just 2-8-0s, and the KCS turned to Lima for ten strikingly modern 2-10-4s with cast underframes, 70-inch drivers and 310-p.s.i. boiler pressure. The 900-909 were delivered in June and July 1937. The 900-904 were oil burners, while the 905-909 were set up to burn coal. The big engines were all kept north of DeQueen, Ark., due to bridge restrictions south of there, and the coal burners were used on the 338 miles between Kansas City and Heavener, Okla., while the oil burners worked south from Heavener 95 miles over the mountain to DeQueen. The reason for the two types of fuel was simply a matter of the relative costs between coal and oil, with readily available locally mined coal on the north end.

The 2-10-4s produced 93,300 pounds of Tractive Effort and could deliver it at track

TEN AWESOME 2-10-4s were delivered by Lima in mid-1937. The coal-burning 905 (above) was at Watts, Ok., in 1942, while the coal-fired 909 and oil-burning 904 (below) posed for a company publicity photo at Pittsburg in 1939. The 2-10-4s had 310-p.s.i boiler pressure, vestibule cabs, 70-inch drivers and cast underframes and huge pilot wheels.

speed. Their 310-p.s.i. boilers were later derated to 300 p.s.i. when the cylinders were developing so much power that they were actually jarring the drivers out of quarter on the axles!

The arrival of the 2-10-4s permitted the retirement of the 0-6-6-0s, although the 2-8-8-0s remained in service. It's remarkable that the only truly modern locomotives on the KCS were usually restricted to only 304 miles of the main line (along with the compound Mallets). The rest of the pre-L&A merger KCS freight service was handled almost exclusively by 2-8-0s, while passenger service was powered by the eleven 800-class Pacifics and a few Ten Wheelers. 🖼

TOP / CHARLES WINTERS / WARREN CAILEFF COLLECTION

KCS PHOTO

SINCE BUCHANAN'S L&A and Edenborn's LR&N had their origins as logging roads, their early power was a bit smaller and lighter than that of the neighboring KCS, though they were all comprised mostly of 4-4-0s, 2-6-0s, 4-6-0s and 2-8-0s. In 1918 the L&A acquired seven powerful but lightweight "Russian Decapods," 2-10-0s that had been built for Russia and then banned from export by the Communist Revolution. The Decapods (100-106) were followed by seven light Baldwin 2-8-2s (551-556) between 1923 and 1927, just prior to the 1928 merger with the LR&N.

Following Harvey Couch's merger of the L&A and LR&N in 1928, in 1930 the greater L&A acquired its first 4-6-2 (309) when it bought Florida East Coast 109. In 1936, at the same time that the KCS was contemplating its 2-10-4s, Harvey Couch was buying five modern 2-8-2s (L&A 561-565) from Lima.

These Mikes weighed 150 tons, compared to a USRA Light Mikado at 145 tons, and they

THE LOUISIANA & ARKANSAS began as a logging road with small locomotives. Number 95 (opposite top), at Shreveport in 1937, was the only one of the LR&N 92-97 Ten-Wheelers not rebuilt into a 392-series (page 15). The 300 (opposite bottom), at Shreveport in 1934, was the first of the L&A's last and largest 4-4-0s. The 500 (below right), at Shreveport in August 1931, sports a Southern valve gear. The 309 (right), at Shreveport in October 1937, is ex-FEC 109 that became the roundhouse boiler in 1939. Mikado 551 (above) was on its way to scrap in 1953. The 562 (bottom) was new from Lima in August 1936; note the tender booster.

had Delta trailing trucks, 240 p.s.i. boilers and 63-inch drivers that delivered 50,200 pounds of T.E. The 561 and 562 had Franklin tender boosters. These would have been modern and useful Mikes on any railroad. That same year, Harvey Couch bought three USRA copy 0-8-0s (L&A 251-253) from the Florida East Coast.

The KCS and L&A were joined October 1939, but their steam engines generally stayed on "home" rails, although there were occasional transfers within the family.

LOUISIANA & ARKANSAS LINES
Route of "The Shreveporter" and "The Hustler"

Louisiana Railway & Navigation Steam Locomotives 1896-1928

Type	Numbers	Built	Driv.	Cyl.	B/P	T.E	Notes
4-4-0	S&RRV 49	Rogers 1864	62"	17x24	130	12,350	Built narrow gauge for NYP&O (Erie); to Edenborn 1897
4-4-0	S&RRV 50-51	??	??	??	??	??	Disposed of 1913-1917
4-4-0	S&RRV 52-54	BLW 1900-01	63"	16x24	180	13,600	Scrapped 1917-34
4-4-0	63	BLW 1904	69"	17x24	180	15,310	Scrapped 1929
2-6-0	S&RRV 55-58	BLW 1901-02	57"	17x24	189	19,650	Disposed 1929-30
2-6-0	60-62	BLW 1904	57"	17x24	180	19,650	Disposed 1924-30
2-6-0	LR&NofT 456	BLW 1900	56"	19x26	190	26,660	Ex-SS&S 13, to MKT 456 to L&A 120; scrapped 1929
2-6-0	LR&NofT 461-462	BLW 1901	56"	19x26	190	26,660	Ex-MKT 461-462; to L&A 124-125; scrapped 1929
2-6-0	123-125	BLW 1900-06	62"	20x28	200	30,200	Ex-MKT 524, 544 and 590; acq. 1924; scrapped 1929
4-6-0	92-97	BLW 1913-15	59"	20x26	180	26,500	Rebuilt to L&A 392-397 1932-38 except 95/395; disposed 1947-50
2-8-0	89	BLW 1900	46"	20x26	180	34,590	Ex-G&SI 19, to LR&N 1911; to LR&N ofT 245 1923; scr. 1934
2-8-0	90-91	BLW 1912	51"	20x26	180	30,780	Sold 1947-48
2-8-0	98-99	BLW 1919	51"	20x26	180	30,780	Sold 1944-47
2-10-0	100-106	BLW 1918	52"	25x28	180	51,500	Russian Decapods acq. 1921 (except 106 1925); disposed 1945-47
0-6-0	S&RRV 59	BLW 190	51"	18X24	160	21,200	Scrapped 1931

NYP&O = New York, Pennsylvania & Ohio / SS&S = Sherman, Shreveport & Southern / G&SI = Gulf & Ship Island

All locomotives on the LR&N and LR&NofT existing in 1928 were transferred to the Louisiana & Arkansas roster.

Louisiana & Arkansas Steam Locomotives 1898-1956

Type	Numbers	Built	Driv.	Cyl.	B/P	T.E	Notes
4-4-0	10-11	??	??	??	??	??	Ex-Arkansas, Louisiana & Southern 10-11; sold 1913
4-4-0	100	BLW 1899	63"	15x22	??	??	Ex-Arkansas, Louisiana & Southern 3; scrapped 1926
4-4-0	101-102	BLW 1894-96	60"	??	??	??	Ex-Bodcaw Lumber 101-102; sold 1910-17
4-4-0	106-108	Alco/Sch, 1893	60"	17x24	??	??	Ex-Chicago & Alton 215, 219, 221; acq 1899-1901; disp. 1909-25
4-4-0	300-303	BLW 1911-12	67"	18x24	200	19,730	Scrapped 1935-41
2-6-0	103	BLW 1898	50"	14x22	??	??	Sold 1910
2-6-0	140-141	BLW 1890	57"	19x24	150	20,648	Ex-CNO&TP 619-620; acq. 1903; sold 1914
4-6-0	104	BLW 1898	??	16x24	??	??	Sold 1910
4-6-0	170-172, 177	BLW 1903-04	63"	20x26	200	22,795	Disposed 1934-50
4-6-0	173-176	BLW 1903-04	57"	20x26	200	27,916	Disposed 1935-37
4-6-0	200-207	BLW 1905-06	57"	20x26	200	31,018	Disposed 1934-47
4-6-0	297	BLW 1915	63"	20x26	200	22,795	Ex-Louisiana & North West 97, acq. 1936; scrapped 1938
4-6-0	392-394, 396-397	BLW 1913-15	69"	19x26	200	23,060	Ex-LR&N 92-94, 96-97, rebuilt 1932-38, disposed 1947-50
4-6-0	95	BLW 1915	59"	20x26	180	26,500	Ex-LR&N 95; scrapped 1947
4-6-0	500-505	BLW 1916-20	57"	22x28	200	40,418	Disposed 1947-53
4-6-0	506-511	BLW 1912-13	57"	22x28	200	40,418	Ex-KCS 400-405; disposed 1947-51
4-6-2	309	Alco/Sch. 1913	69"	20x26	200	28,300	Ex-FEC 109, acq. 1930; boiler to Shreveport roundhouse 1939
4-6-2	800, 806	Alco/Sch. 1912	75"	24x28	225	41,175	Ex-KCS 800, 806, transferred 1940; scrapped 1952-53
2-8-0	150	BLW 1904	56"	19x26	200	25,327	Ex-Louisiana & North West 10; sold 1922
2-8-0	425-429	BLW 1901	60"	21x30	200	37,485	Ex-Colorado Midland 201-205, acq. 1920; disposed 1933-49
2-8-0	490-491, 494, 526	BLW 1906-08	55"	22x30	210	47,124	Ex-KCS same numbers; acquired 1939-40; disposed 1952
2-8-0	559-560	BLW 1913	57"	25x30	200	57,948	Ex-KCS 559-560, acquired 1940; scrapped 1952
2-8-2	544	Alco/Sch. 1928	57"	23x28	200	45,000	Ex=Natchez, Columbia & Mobile 204; acq. 1931, scr. 1953
2-8-2	551-556	BLW 1923-27	57"	24x28	200	48,100	Scrapped 1952-53
2-8-2	561-565	Lima 1936	63"	23x32	240	50,200	561-562 with Franklin tender truck booster; disposed 1952-54
0-8-0	251-253	Richmond 1924	50"	25x28	180	52,500	USRA copy 0-8-0; ex-FEC 251-253; acq. 1936; disp. 1954-56
0-8-0	1007	BLW 1903	56"	21x30	210	42,937	Ex-KCS 1007, rebuilt 2-8-0, transferred 1940; scrapped 1950

Louisiana, Arkansas & Texas Steam Locomotives 1923-1950

Type	Numbers	Built	Driv.	Cyl.	B/P	T.E	Notes
2-6-0	455-456, 461-462	BLW 1900-01	56"	19x26	190	26,600	Ex-MK&T same nos.; 456, 461-462 to LR&N; 455 scr. 1944
4-6-0	231, 233	BLW 1905	68"	19x26	200	23,400	Ex-MK&T same numbers; scrapped 1933-34
4-6-0	239-240	Alco/Sch. 1907	68"	19x26	200	23,100	Ex-MK&T same numbers; scrapped 1933
2-8-0	241-243	Brooks 1903	56"	21x28	190	38,000	Ex-BR&P 262, 301, 311; acq. 1924; scrapped 1935-50
2-8-0	671-675	Alco/Sch. 190	60"	20x30	190	33,400	Ex-MK&T 438-442; scrapped 1940-41

MK&T = Missouri, Kansas & Texas / BR&P = Buffalo, Rochester & Pittsburgh

Rosters compiled by Harold K. Vollrath from official sources

In the early 1950s the L&A sent its three ex-Florida East Coast 0-8-0s (purchased in 1936) to the KCS. The 251 and 253 were put to work on transfer runs and yard jobs in Kansas City, while the 252 wound up in Greenville, Texas.

They were among the last steam operations on the KCS. In the spring of 1954, the 253, still wearing its LOUISIANA & ARKANSAS lettering, was moved to DeQueen, Ark., where it became the last steam engine in service on the system. In the summer of 1954 it was replaced by the lone Baldwin VO660 switcher 1150.

THE THREE LOUISIANA & ARKANSAS ex-FEC 0-8-0s were moved to the KCS in the early 1950s. The 251 (above) was alongside the Kaw River easing out of the Santa Fe's Argentine Yard on July 28, 1953, and the 253 was at Argentine (below) on February 1, 1954. A short while later the 253 was assigned to DeQueen, Ark., where it became the last steam locomotive in service on the entire KCS system in the summer of 1954. Note the L&A lettering.

CHAPTER 3

JIM BOYD COLLECTION

NUMBER 1 was renumbered 21 in December 1942 and equipped with the induction trainphone antenna in 1944. By July 1961, when the E3 paused at Neosho, Mo., on the southbound *Southern Belle*, the paint scheme had been simplified by eliminating the "mating" arc at the rear of the carbody sides.

Compare with pages 16, 17 and 31, and the heavily retouched June 1940 publicity photo (below). The left-pointing nose herald was soon "corrected" to point to the right (page 16). The images of "Miss Southern Belle" and the New Orleans ironwork (opposite) were used extensively in advertising.

HARVEY COUCH was quick to commit his newly merged KCS and L&A to diesel power with the *Southern Belle* streamliner in 1940. He had hosted Electro-Motive's E3 demonstrator 822 in the summer of 1938 and purchased the unit in July 1939 along with a second E3. The two units were delivered in a red, black and yellow lightning stripe livery (**page 15**) with a *Flying Crow* nose herald.

When the *Southern Belle* livery was finalized, the two E3s (KCS 1 and 2) were returned to EMC at

KCS PHOTO

La Grange, Illinois, where they were repainted into the new yellow, red and "*Belle* green" livery. The demonstrator's flush headlight had been modified to the new standard cowled headlight when delivered as KCS No.1 in the *Flying Crow* livery, and both the 1 and 2 returned from La Grange in June 1940 with a second headlight added beneath the first. An oscillating light was placed in the upper casing, while the fixed headlight was moved to the lower one.

It had become obvious that two units would not

Dieselizing the KCS / L&A

TILLIE CAILEFF

have been able to cover the *Southern Belle* schedule, which required three trainsets, and a third E3 (KCS 3) was delivered on June 20, 1940, along with the repainted 1 and 2. The trio arrived with a circular nose herald with a left-pointing arrow (**page 29**) which was apparently perceived as incorrect and soon revised to a right-pointing arrow (**page 14**).

The *Southern Belle* was inaugurated on September 1, 1940, and the KCS and L&A were in the diesel streamliner business. Obviously impressed by the potential of the

E-units in their temporary stint on the *Flying Crow*, the KCS soon placed an order for two more, which by now had designated model E6.

After the custom E4 for the Seaboard Air Line in October 1938 and the "standard" E3 in March 1939, EMC decided to standardize its catalog 2000-h.p. passenger unit with the twin 12-cylinder 567 engines as the E6 in November 1939 (although it did deliver some custom E5s for the CB&Q in February 1940 that had been abuilding before the E6 was made standard). All four models were mechanically

DAVID GRAEFF

NUMBER 24, one of the two E6s delivered in January 1942, was on northbound No.16 at Cedar Grove in August 1963 (left), entering Shreveport with an Illinois Central coach and heavyweight Pullman, likely to handle a troop movement from Fort Polk. On April 27, 1955, the two *Flying Crows*, northbound 16 out of Port Arthur and southbound 15, were scheduled to meet at Many, La., 76 miles south of Shreveport, at 2:20 p.m. Here 16 with E6 25 is in the siding (opposite bottom) while 15, with sister E6 24, holds the main and accelerates out of town (below) as 15 eases up to the north switch (bottom) to resume its run to Kansas City.

essentially identical. The Electro-Motive Corporation and Winton Engine Company were both subsidiaries of General Motors, and on January 1, 1941, they were formally merged to become the new Electro-Motive Division of GM, headquartered at the huge new locomotive factory in La Grange, Illinois, a southwestern suburb of Chicago.

KCS E6s 4 and 5 were on the erecting floor at La Grange on December 7, 1941, and were delivered to the railroad in January 1942 in the same livery as the E3s but with the right-facing nose herald arrow. Shortly thereafter, the War Production Board stopped production of any passenger-only diesels.

To avoid confusion between locomotive and train numbers, in December 1942 the E-units were renumbered from 1-5 to 21-25. ◙

A.E. BROWN / WARREN CAILEFF COLLECTION

THE FUTURE OF KCS passenger service was predicted with the inauguration in September 1940 of the *Southern Belle,* and any future passenger locomotives would be diesels. Three E3s and three NW2 switchers (1100, delivered in May 1939 and 1101-1102 in September 1941) were on the roster on December 7, 1941, and, fortunately, two new EMD E6s (Nos. 4 and 5) were already on order when hostilities commenced. The E6s were delivered in January 1942 before restrictions were clamped on the construction of any new passenger diesels. By then, two more EMD NW2 switchers (L&A 1125-1126) had been added to the roster in January 1942.

The wartime traffic surge postponed the planned retirement of the 2-8-8-0s, and the 758, 759, 762 and 764 were modernized at the Pittsburg Shop and rebuilt as simple articulateds

with high pressure (upped to 250 p.s.i.) boiler steam going directly to all four cylinders. The remaining 757-766 engines got the increased boiler pressure but remained compounds.

Suddenly in dire need of more heavy road power, in 1942 the KCS was able to buy six drag-era Wabash 2-10-2s that became KCS 200-205 and four USRA Light 2-10-2s from the Ann Arbor (KCS 220-223). Additionally, engines were leased from the C&NW (four 2-8-2s),

KCS PHOTO / RAILFAN & RAILROAD MAGAZINE COLLECTION

IN APRIL 1943 2-10-4 905 (above) and numerous switchers got War Bonds billboards on their tenders. Ann Arbor USRA Light 2-10-2 2552 became KCS 222 (top) in 1942. Four of the 2-8-8-0 Mallets were rebuilt simple like the 758 (below).

WARREN CAILEFF COLLECTION

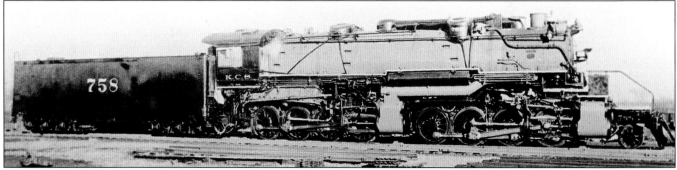

THREE EMC E3 PASSENGER UNITS and two E6s were on the roster by early 1942, along with five NW2s. The first E6, renumbered 24 in December 1942, was at Texarkana (above) **in December 1947 on No.16, the northbound** *Flying Crow*. **The first diesel purchased by the KCS (May 1939) was EMC NW2 1100. It was at Kansas City** (below) **in April 1967.**

Monon (three 2-10-2s, two Mikados, a Pacific and an 0-6-0), Chicago Great Western (three 2-8-0s), Frisco (two each 4-6-0s, 2-8-0s and 0-6-0s) and C&EI (three each 2-8-0s and 0-6-0s). All the leased engines were returned by 1945.

Remarkably, while all the steam leasing was going on, the War Production Board allocated four Alco RS1 road switchers to the KCS. The 1110-1113 were outshopped between November 23 and December 1, 1943. These were the KCS's first freight units capable of multiple-unit operation, but they were generally used as heavy switchers. The wartime traffic grew rapidly, and the KCS struggled to keep up.

Diesel Switchers

While the elegant passenger units were grabbing the headlines, they were not the first diesels on the KCS or L&A. Although in the spring of 1939 the E3 demonstrator 822 was the first diesel to operate on the KCS, the first diesel owned by the KCS was an unassuming black NW2 switcher numbered 1100. Electro-Motive had introduced its first standard switchers powered by the 567 engine with the 6-cylinder 600-h.p. SW1 in January 1939 and the 12-cylinder 1000-h.p. NW2 in February.

The 1100 was outshopped on May 26, 1939, and arrived on the property in a simple black standard EMC switcher livery with white frame and hood stripes and a cab side number. It had friction bearings, two short stacks and no multiple-unit (m.u.) equipment. The stacks were soon replaced with EMD's new taller standard stacks. Over the years, the hood stripe was eliminated and replaced by painting the handrails white, and a bright red and white herald was added on the cab.

In mid-September 1941 NW2s 1101 and 1102, identical to the 1100, were added to the KCS roster. In January 1942 these were followed by 1125 and 1126 for the L&A that carried full LOUISIANA & ARKANSAS lettering on their hoods.

THE KCS FOLLOWED up its first NW2 1000 of May 1939 (page 31) with two more, 1101 and 1102, in September 1941. The veteran 1101 (left) was working an unidentified location in July 1968 with spark arrestor stacks. Sister 1102 (top) was at Kansas City on September 4, 1966. Two NW2s, 1125 and 1126, were delivered to the L&A in January 1942. None of the NW2s were m.u. equipped.

FOUR ALCO RS1 ROAD SWITCHERS were delivered to the KCS in late November 1943. "Class engine" 1100 was at Kansas City (above) on September 4, 1966, in its factory livery that included the hood stripe and cab-side herald.

Sister 1101 (top), in Kansas City in May 1968, sported a simplified livery. The four RS1s (1110-1113) were initially used on Texas lines locals, but they all ended up in Kansas City transfer and yard service until retired in 1967 and '68.

Wartime Alco Road Switchers

In May 1940 Alco put its new "low profile" 6-cylinder 539 diesel engine into a pair of end-cab switchers that would become long-lived best sellers, the normally aspirated 660-h.p. S1 and turbocharged 1000-h.p. S2. In March 1941 Schenectady placed that 1000-h.p. engine on a longer underframe and added a short hood behind the cab for a steam generator. The unit was placed on road trucks good for 60 m.p.h. and equipped with motor field shunting appropriate for road speeds. With the addition of m.u. equipment, the end result was the first true road switcher, later dubbed the RS1.

After delivering the first pair of RS1s to the Rock Island, whose president, John Farrington, was reportedly instrumental in creating the road switcher idea, Alco outshopped a total of 13 "pre-war" RS1s for the Atlanta & St. Andrews Bay, Tennessee Coal & Iron, Milwaukee Road

THE ONLY RS1 to get the 1960s red livery was 1112, which was at Knoche Yard in Kansas City (above) in May 1968, only four months before it was traded to EMD along with sisters 1111 and 1113. The 1113 (below) was still in factory livery on a transfer at Kansas City Union Station in July 1963. The RS1s had m.u. receptacles but no end walk-over ramps.

and New York, Susquehanna & Western by June 1942. The units were so effective that the entire production to date was "drafted" by the U.S. Army for use on the Trans-Iranian Railway in the Soviet Union. The reclaimed RS1s were refitted with six-wheel C-C trucks and low profile "export" cabs before shipment overseas. The Army got 44 more modified RS1s between November 1942 and February 1943.

Domestic production resumed in April 1943 under War Production Board allocations, and 16 RS1s were built (for the A&StAB, NYS&W, Milwaukee Road, Rock Island and Banberger) before four were authorized for the KCS. The KCS had no plan to dieselize, and the WPB allocation was probably a result of the railroad's frantic search for leasable steam power.

The 1110-1113 were not all that useful for heavy wartime traffic. In pairs, they were not powerful or fast enough for road work, and the fleet was too small to permit lash-ups of three or four units on a regular basis. They soon settled in to work in pairs on the Texas line locals and singly in Shreveport and New Orleans transfer service, where they served

TWO PHOTOS / JIM BOYD

throughout the war. The RS1s were the only diesels ordered and acquired by the KCS during the war years.

Following the postwar diesel boom, in 1954 the RS1s found a permanent home in the Kansas City terminal district. Rugged and reliable, though somewhat under-powered, the RS1s churned around Kansas City until the 1110 was sold for scrap in February 1967 and the remaining trio was traded to EMD on SD40s in September 1968.

The "Joint Agency"

The potential influx of wartime traffic posed a severe problem for the Milwaukee Road's line into Kansas City, since it had a very poor bridge with steep and curving approaches over the Missouri River entering the Northeast

BILL G. SHARP

THE INDUCTION TRAINPHONE ANTENNA shows clearly atop E6 No.25 on No.15 at Texarkana. The Aireon Corporation system was installed in 1944.

Industrial District and a cramped Coberg Yard near the KCS roundhouse. There had been proposals since 1935 to move the Milwaukee into the KCS East Yard, and the war emergency prompted construction of a new bridge and a new line into the east end of the KCS yard.

On May 1, 1942, the KCS and Milwaukee Road created the "Joint Agency" to handle its combined terminal operations, centered at the KCS East Yard (later named Knoche Yard). The new bridge (now the Truman Bridge) was not finished until 1945, but combined KCS and Milwaukee operations began immediately. The Joint Agency did its own customer billing

and allocated expense charges and work assignments between the two railroads.

E3 Phone Home

In 1942 the Pennsylvania Railroad introduced the first practical railroad "radio" system. The Motorola system was actually an induction telephone system that transmitted only a short distance from the locomotive or caboose to a paralleling lineside phone wire. Since the system used an "overlay" frequency, it could utilize existing telephone and telegraph lines without interfering with their primary function. The vacuum-tube onboard telephone equipment broadcast to the lineside wires through long antennas mounted atop the locomotive or caboose.

The KCS was eager to employ a similar system and in 1944 began to install phones developed by the Aireon Corp. of Kansas City. The onboard systems had loudspeakers for "hailing" and telephone handsets for the actual conversation. While used primarily for engine-caboose communication, the system also put trains in touch with lineside station operators within about a 25-mile range.

While the system permitted communication with dispatchers, it was used for "information only," and issuing operating instructions or train orders was specifically forbidden, except in emergency. The KCS was a "dark railroad" in the 1940s, with some segments of block signals, and all operations were by timetable and train orders.

The induction trainphone was improved over the years, with a small whip antenna added to separate the transmitting and receiving functions, while retaining the rooftop "handrails." (A Pennsy fan once observed, "It's not a question why cab units had handrails on their roofs, but why road switchers have induction trainphone antennas along the sides of their frames.")

The KCS used the induction trainphones until mid-1960, when it was replaced with a "modern" radio system. The only other major railroads to use an induction system were the Pennsy and Duluth, Missabe & Iron Range.

KCS / L&A Diesel Fleet 1939-1973

No.	Re#	RR	Model	Built	Re# 4/73 – Notes (All 00A and 00D cab units re# 1/1/57)
1100		KCS	NW2	EMC 5/26/39	First diesel owned by KCS/L&A; rebuilt as slug 200 10/69
1	21	KCS	E3	EMC 9/13/38	Ex-EMC demonstrator 822; to KCS 7/31/39; re# 21 12/2/42; sold for scrap 1/64
2	22	KCS	E3	EMC 7/31/39	Re# 22 12/3/42; sold for scrap 11/64
3	23	KCS	E3	EMC 6/20/40	Re# 23 11/30/42; wrecked, rebuilt by EMD 1/52 as 2000-h.p. **E8m 23**; sold C&NW 1/28/70
1101-1102		KCS	NW2	EMD 9/19/41	To C&NW 1005 and 1006 via PNC 7/71
4	24	KCS	E6	EMD 1/10/42	Re# 24 12/4/42; sold for scrap 11/64
5	25	KCS	E6	EMD 1/16/42	Re# 25 12/1/42; rebuilt by EMD 6/59 as 2000-h.p. **E9m 25**; sold C&NW 1/28/70
1125-1126		L&A	NW2	EMD 1/16/42	Disposed 9/85-12/86
1110-1113		KCS	RS1	Alco 11/2342	Disposed 2/67-9/68
1150		KCS	VO660	BLW 5/8/46	To PNC 7/65 for scrap
1200-1203		KCS	NW2	EMD 10/31/46	**KCS 4200-4203**: disposed 8/83-9/85
60A	60	KCS	Erie A	FM 11/30/46	Repowered 1750-h.p. 16-567C by EMD 12/56; to EMD 11/66
60B, 61B		KCS	Eric B	FM 11/30/46	Repowered 1750-h.p. 16-567C by EMD 1/58 and 8/55; to EMD 11-12/66
61A	61	KCS	Erie A	FM 11/30/46	Repowered 1750-h.p. 16-567C by EMD 5/56; to EMD 11/66
1204-1211		KCS	NW2	EMD 12/28/46	1204 scrapped 1972; 1205-1211 to **KCS 4205-4211**: disposed 9/85
50A	50	KCS	F3A	EMD 1/10/47	Wrecked 9/70, scrapped
50B, 50C		KCS	F3B	EMD 1/10/47	To EMD 9/71 via PNC
50D	77	KCS	F3A	EMD 1/10/47	To EMD 5/63
51A	51	KCS	F3A	EMD 1/13/47	To EMD 9/68
51B, 51C		KCS	F3B	EMD 1/13/47	Disposed 6/72-3/80
51D	78	KCS	F3A	EMD 1/13/47	To EMD 5/63
60C	63	KCS	Erie A	FM 1/31/47	Repowered 1750-h.p. 16-567C by EMD 9/55; to EMD 12/66
61C	64	KCS	Erie A	FM 1/31/47	Repowered 1750-h.p. 16-567C by EMD 9/55; to EMD 12/66
52A	52	KCS	F3A	EMD 5/9/47	To EMD 12/66
52B, 52C		KCS	F3B	EMD 5/10/47	To EMD 9/68 and 8/63
52D	79	KCS	F3A	EMD 5/12/47	To EMD 8/63
53A	53	KCS	F3A	EMD 5/13/47	To EMD 8/63
53B, 53C		KCS	F3B	EMD 5/20/47	To EMD 8/72 and 9/68
53D	80	KCS	F3A	EMD 5/20/47	To EMD 8/72 via PNC
54A	94	KCS	F3A	EMD 5/19/47	**KCS 4051**; sold for scrap 9/86
54B, 54C		KCS	F3B	EMD 5/19/47	To PNC 4/72 and 6/70
54D	81	KCS	F3A	EMD 5/19/47	To EMD 5/63
62A	62	L&A	Erie A	FM 6/23/47	Passenger equipped; repowered 1750-h.p. 16-567C by EMD 5/56; sold for scrap 1/64
62C	65	L&A	Erie A	FM 6/23/47	Passenger equipped; new FM prime mover 4/53; sold for scrap 11/62
30A	30	KCS	F3A	EMD 11/12/47	**KCS 4050**; passenger equipped; sold Central California Railroad Museum 4/24/89
30B		KCS	F3B	EMD 11/12/47	Passenger equipped; to EMD 8/72 via PNC
31A	31	KCS	F3A	EMD 11/12/47	Passenger equipped; to EMD 9/68
31B		KCS	F3B	EMD 11/12/47	Passenger equipped; to PNC 6/72
55A	55	L&A	F3A	EMD 3/8/48	To EMD 9/68
55B, 55C		L&A	F3B	EMD 3/8/48	To EMD 12/66 and via PNC 9/71
55D	82	L&A	F3A	EMD 3/8/48	To EMD 5/63
56A	56	L&A	F3A	EMD 3/8/48	To EMD 8/63
56B, 56C		L&A	F3B	EMD 3/8/48	56B rebuilt to road slug 201 12/17/69; 56C sold for scrap 3/80
56D	83	L&A	F3A	EMD 3/8/48	To EMD 9/71
57A	57	L&A	F3A	EMD 3/10/48	To EMD 8/63
57B, 57C		L&A	F3B	EMD 3/10/48	To PNC 10/74 and to EMD 10/70 via PNC
57D	84	L&A	F3A	EMD 3/10/48	To EMD 6/72 via PNC
58A	58	L&A	F3A	EMD 3/11/48	Re# **L&A 95** in 5/68; **L&A 4052**: sold for scrap 9/86
58B, 58C		L&A	F3B	EMD 3/11/48	To EMD 9/68 and 9/71 via PNC and via PNC 9/71
58D	85	L&A	F3A	EMD 3/8/48	**L&A 4053**; sold for scrap 9/86
62B		L&A	Erie B	FM 4/20/48	Repowered 1750-h.p. 16-567C by EMD 10/56; to EMD 11/66
1212-1221		KCS	NW2	EMD 5/11/48	**L&A 4212-/-4221** (1216, 1218 1220 sold 1972, not re#); disposed 3/72-9/89
59A	59	L&A	F5A	EMD 10/28/48	EMD testbed 951, built 3/48; to EMD 7/63
32A	32	L&A	F7A	EMD 2/17/49	EMD's first F7; passenger equipped; wrecked 9/70, sold for scrap
32B		L&A	F7A	EMD 2/17/49	Passenger equipped; to EMD 8/72 via PNC
33A	33	L&A	F7A	EMD 2/17/49	Passenger equipped; to PNC 6/72
40		L&A	H15-44	FM 5/21/49	Scrapped 1/64 (Both 40 and 41 were passenger-equipped and long-hood forward.)
41	45	L&A	H15-44	FM 5/21/49	Repowered 1750-h.p. 16-567C by EMD 4/15/58; re# 45 3/67; to PNC 3/71, then EMD
33B		L&A	F7B	EMD 10/19/49	Passenger equipped; to EMD 8/72 via PNC
70A	70	KCS	F7A	EMD 10/19/49	**KCS 4055**: retired 7/88
70B		KCS	F7B	EMD 10/19/49	Sold for scrap 9/86
70C	87	KCS	F7A	EMD 10/19/49	**KCS 4056**:
1222-1226		KCS	NW2	EMD 10/19/49	**KCS 4222-4226**; disposed beginning 9/85
71A	71	KCS	F7A	EMD 10/20/49	**KCS 4057**: sold Mountain Diesel 4/88
71B		KCS	F7B	EMD 10/20/49	To EMD 8/72 via PNC

CONTINUED ON NEXT PAGE

THE SECOND WORLD WAR ended with Japan's surrender aboard the battleship *Missouri* in Tokyo Bay on September 2, 1945, and the KCS was eager to dieselize as quickly as locomotives could be ordered and delivered. But that was the rub. Every other railroad in the country had the same idea, and the diesel builders were overwhelmed with orders. The first delivery that the KCS was able to secure was a single 660-h.p. VO660 switcher from Baldwin. Although owned by the KCS, the 1150 was put into service on the Louisiana, Arkansas & Texas at Greenville on May 8, 1946. The little four-stacker was powered

Diesels After the War

No.	Re#	RR	Model	Built	Re# 4/73 – Notes (All 00A and 00D cab units re# 1/1/57)
71C	88	KCS	F7A	EMD 10/20/49	**KCS 4059**: sold for scrap 9/86
59B, 59C		KCS	F7B	EMD 8/26/50	Both copnverted to slugs 1/1/77; **KCS 4077, 4078**
59D	86	KCS	F7A	EMD 8/26/50	**KCS 4054**; to Central California RR Museum 4/24/89
72A	72	KCS	F7A	EMD 8/29/50	To EMD 12/72 via PNC
72B-72C		KCS	F7B	EMD 8/29/50	72B sold for scrap 4/80; 72C to EMD 9/68
72D	89	KCS	F7A	EMD 8/29/50	Sold to PNC 9/74
73A	73	KCS	F7A	EMD 8/30/50	To Wilson Railway Supply 4/89
73B-73C		KCS	F7B	EMD 8/30/50	73B sold for scrap 9/86; 73C to EMD 9/58
73D	90	KCS	F7A	EMD 8/30/50	Converted to slug **KCS 4060** 4/78
75B-75C		KCS	F7B	EMD 8/31/50	75C converted to slug **KCS 4075**: 75B to EMD via PNC 9/71
74A	74	L&A	F7A	EMD 9/1/50	To EMD 11/68
74B-74C		L&A	F7B	EMD 9/1/50	To EMD via PNC 12/72 and 9/72
1300-1309		KCS	SW7	EMD 10/28/50	**KCS 4300-4309**; disposed 9/85
1310-1315		L&A	SW7	EMD 1/11/51	**L&A 4310-4315**; disposed 9/85-3/88
74D	91	L&A	F7A	EMD 2/27/51	**L&A 4061**: sold to Mountain Diesel 4/88
75A	75	L&A	F7A	EMD 2/27/51	**L&A 4062**: sold for scrap 12/86
76B-76C		L&A	F7B	EMD 2/27/51	76B wrecked 12/8/67, to EMD via PNC 10/70
75D	92	L&A	F7A	EMD 2/28/51	To EMD via PNC 9/71
77B		L&A	F7B	EMD 2/28/51	To PNC 10/74
1160-1163		L&A	S12	BLW 4/10/51	Traded to EMD on SD40s 9/26/68
76A	76	L&A	F7A	EMD 4/20/51	**L&A 4063**: to Mountain Diesel 4/88
77C		L&A	F7B	EMD 4/20/51	To EMD 8/72 via PNC
78B-78C		L&A	F7B	EMD 4/20/51	To EMD via PNC 8/72 and 11/72
79B		L&A	F7B	EMD 4/21/51	To EMD 8/72 via PNC
76D	93	L&A	F7A	EMD 4/21/51	**L&A 4064**: to Wilson Railway Supply 4/89
150-154		L&A	GP7	EMD 11/6/51	Short hood forward. Disposed 8/82-
23		KCS	E8m	EMC 6/20/40	Built as E3 No.3; **rebuilt by EMD 1/52** as 2000-h.p. **E8m**; sold C&NW 1/28/70
26-29		KCS	E8A	EMD 1/31/52	Disposed 3/68-1/70
155		L&A	GP7	EMD 2/20/53	Short hood forward; **L&A 4150-4154**; sold for scrap 4/87
156-162		KCS	GP7	EMD 2/23/53	Short hood forward; **KCS 4155-4162**; disposed beginning 9/85
1120		L&A	HH900	Alco 10/21/37	Ex-Youngstown & Northern 211, **acquired 4/56**; sold K.C. Public Service Co. 7/64
1121-1123		L&A	HH1000	Alco 2/27/40	Manufacturers Railway 201-203, **acquired 4/56**; to EMD 11/66, 9/68 and 12/66
163-165		KCS	GP9	EMD 6/4/59	Short hood forward; **KCS 4163-4165**; disposed beginning 9/83
25		KCS	E9m	EMD 1/16/42	Built as E6 No.5; **rebuilt by EMD 6/59** as 2000-h.p. **E9m**; sold C&NW 1/28/70
100-109		KCS	GP30	EMD 5/9/62	Dynamic brakes; first units delivered in red; **KCS 4100-4109**; disposed beginning 1986
20		KCS	E7A	EMD 7/7/48	Ex-Maine Central 709, **acquired 9/62**; to EMD 9/68
110-119		KCS	GP30	EMD 7/24/63	Dynamic brakes; **KCS 4110-4119**; disposed beginniing 1986
6		L&A	E7A	EMD 6/46	Ex-Maine Central 705, **acquired 11/63**; to PNC 11/69
7, 11, 12		KCS	E7A	EMD 6/46	Ex-MEC 706,707 and 708, **acquired 11/63**; 7 and 11 to EMD 9/68; 12 to PNC 11/68
600-613		KCS	SD40	EMD 10/13/66	Dynamic brakes; 600 first unit painted white
1500-1503		KCS	SW1500	EMD 11/12/66	**KCS 4320-4323**
1114		KCS	S2	Alco 10/31/40	Ex-Kansas City Terminal 51, **acquired 2/20/67** from PNC; returned 6/1/71
1504-1517		KCS	SW1500	EMD 8/8/68	**KCS 4324-4337**; 1512 to scrap 4/87
614-621		KCS	SD40	EMD 8/9/68	Dynamic brakes
622-627		KCS	SD40	EMD 5/15/70	Dynamic brakes; returned to lessor 6/15/85, to Soo Line 6400-6405
628-636		KCS	SD40	EMD 3/18/71	Dynamic brakes
1518-1531		KCS	SW1500	EMD 4/26/71	**KCS 4338-4351**
1532-1541		KCS	SW1500	EMD 2/3/72	**KCS 4352-4361**
637-656		KCS	SD40-2	EMD 2/3/72	Dynamic brakes; 637 EMD's first SD40-2

Roster compiled by Jim Boyd from numerous sources.

by a 6-cylinder normally aspirated de la Vergne engine and was the last VO660 built before Baldwin upgraded to its "600-series" engine.

The lone VO turned out to be somewhat maintenance-prone and was soon moved to Kansas City. In 1956 it was leased out to the Pure Oil Company refinery in Lake Charles, La., before finding a final home at DeQueen, Ark., doing the light duties that had been the last steam assignment on the KCS. In 1963 the orphan Baldwin was replaced at DeQueen with six-year-older high hood Alco HH1000! Alco 1122 (**page 71**) was purchased second-hand from the Manufacturers Railway in 1956. The Baldwin was finally scrapped in July 1965.

"The Kansas City Southern also has ordered five 6000-h.p. diesel-electric freight locomotives, twelve diesel-electric switching locomotives and two 3000-h.p. diesel-electric passenger locomotives from the Electro-Motive Division of General Motors Corporation, together with new streamlined aluminum passenger cars of the latest type from the Pullman-Standard Manufacturing Company and the American Car & Foundry Company. Delivery is expected about the middle of 1947.

"All of the new road freight and passenger locomotives will be equipped with radiophone, for communication between engine and caboose and with other trains and wayside stations. The equipment is being purchased from the Aireon Manufacturing Corporation of Kansas City.

"The entire railroad equipment purchase program calls

EMERY GULASH

The Press Release

The announcement from KCS Advertising Manager C.H. Taylor, dated August 17, 1946, proclaimed the railroad's dieselization plans:

"What probably is the world's largest and most powerful diesel-electric has been ordered by the Kansas City Southern Lines according to a joint announcement today by W.N. Deramus, president of the railway, and R.H. Morse, Jr., vice president and general sales manager of the Fairbanks-Morse Company of Chicago, the builders.

"The streamlined 8000-h.p. rail goliath will have a maximum speed of 65 miles per hour and will be used in the mountainous section of the railway between Pittsburg, Kan., and DeQueen, Arkansas. Delivery is expected in November."

After explaining the details of the opposed-piston power plant, the press release continued:

for a total investment of approximately $7,000,000."

Switchers Arrive First

As referenced in the August 17, 1946, press release, the KCS got the first of its postwar EMDs, four 1000-h.p. NW2s, between October 31 and November 11, 1946, beating out the "world's largest and most powerful" by almost a month. Switchers 1200-1203 were essentially identical to the four (KCS 1100-1101, L&A 1125-1126) that had arrived in September 1941 and January 1942. Although the new units had tall stacks, they retained the "stepped" hood slope in front of the cab, friction-bearing trucks and no m.u. Beginning on December 28, the remaining eight NW2s of the twelve mentioned press release (1204-1211) arrived on the property.

WARREN CAILEFF

THE FIRST DIESEL acquired by the KCS after the war was a single Baldwin VO660. The 1150 worked first on the L&A at Greenville, Texas, but soon moved to Kansas City. After lease in 1956 to the Pure Oil refinery at Lake Charles, La., the little Baldwin was assigned to DeQueen, Ark., where a switcher was needed for only a few hours a day. It was at the Shreveport shop (above) on May 22, 1965, just two months before being sold to Precision National for scrap. The first postwar EMD on the KCS, NW2 1200, delivered on Halloween 1946, was in the 1960s red livery at Kansas City (opposite) in June 1965 with a Milwaukee Road transfer caboose, typical of the Joint Agency operations.

Freight Units from Erie

Switch engines were fine and useful, but what the KCS really needed were the road diesels to relieve the Mallets and Consolidations. The order books were backed up two years at

JIM BOYD

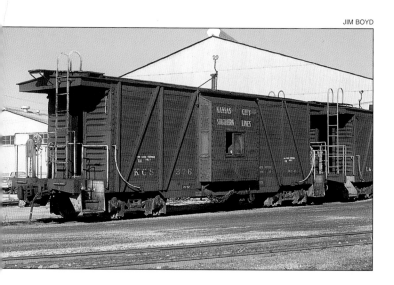

THE KCS PITTSBURG SHOP began a program in 1940 of building bay window cabooses from steel-framed outside-braced composite boxcars. The KCS 376, at New Orleans in March 1971, rides on Allied full cushion express trucks that were used during the war on troop sleepers. The L&A Minden Shop also had a similar caboose-building program.

La Grange, but Fairbanks-Morse of Beloit, Wis., had been able to offer almost immediate delivery of its new 2000-h.p. dual-service cab units that were each powered by a 10-cylinder opposed-piston diesel engine. They were two-cycle normally aspirated engines that operated on the same principle as the EMD 567 but had ten vertical inline cylinders with a crankshaft on both the top and the bottom. From each crankshaft, a rod and piston reached into the cylinder from both top and bottom. Fuel injection and combustion took place in the center between the pistons, creating what was in reality a 20-cylinder engine.

Although the "O.P." had been designed in 1939 as a locomotive engine, it was installed in only six Southern Railway motor cars (800-h.p. 5 cylinder) before FM engine production was redirected to the U.S. Navy for marine power plants, particularly in submarines. The first "real" locomotive built by FM was Milwaukee Road 1000-h.p. switcher 1802 in August 1944.

FM had hired the renowned industrial designer Raymond Leowy to style the huge carbody for the 2000-h.p. unit, and he did an impressive job. The locomotive was too large

DON BALL

for the Beloit erecting floor, however, and they were assembled at the General Electric plant in Erie, Pa. – resulting in the name "Erie Built."

Although four of the big GE traction motors could handle the 2000 h.p. output, the sheer size and weight of the units mandated six-wheel trucks of the A1A configuration, with one traction motor on each outer axle and a non-powered idler axle in the center – the same motor arrangement used on the EMD E-units. (Ol' Leonor Loree must have turned over in his grave when his masterpiece 2-8-8-0s were to be replaced by diesels that wasted one-third of their weight on idler axles!)

Fairbanks-Morse had announced the Erie Built in 1945 and delivered a passenger version to the Union Pacific in December 1945. The second group went to the Milwaukee Road in October 1946. One month later, the KCS got the third group of Erie Builts and the first units specifically intended for freight service.

The initial delivery was a single A-B-B-A set, numbered KCS 60A-60B-61B-61A, that was outshopped on November 30, 1946. This was followed on January 31, 1947, with two more cab units, KCS 60C and 61C, that gave the railroad two A-B-A road sets. While the KCS eagerly tried the 8000-h.p. four unit set (equaling the power of three 2-10-4s!), it quickly concluded that two 6000-h.p. sets were more practical for operations on a 1947 railroad.

The yellow, red and *Belle* green E-unit livery had been created by the GM Styling Section in 1940. As mentioned in the August 1946 press release, the KCS had by that time placed orders for cab-and-booster freight and passenger units. A new livery was apparently desired for the freight units, and somewhere in the process it was decided to keep the basic *Belle* scheme and simply reverse the red and yellow for the freight units and change the dark *Belle* green to black.

JIM BOYD

A THREE-UNIT SET of Erie Builts was crossing the Highway U.S.50 overpass (left) at Eastwood Hills on the southeast side of Kansas City around 1956. Prior to January 1957, the dispatchers and crews could arbitrarily assign engine numbers in the indicator boards, and this lead unit could not have been 62A or 62C, both of which had a different windshield (page 46). The 61 (built as 61A) was in the Kansas City Knoche Yard engine terminal (above) in August 1965 alongside a Milwaukee Alco S4 switcher.

The KCS had its orders on the books in mid-1946 at both EMD and Fairbanks-Morse, and the EMD Styling Section was undoubtedly involved in modifying the paint scheme. The first units delivered in the new livery, however, were the Erie Builts. And although the first publicity photo of the Erie Builts showed dual headlights (**below**), the units were actually delivered with the single headlights that would become standard for all KCS freight diesels.

FAIRBANKS-MORSE

FAIRBANKS-MORSE and the KCS used this airbrushed photo to publicize the "8000-h.p. world's largest locomotive." The October 1947 *Railroad Magazine* observed in a photo caption that it "… hauled freight between Pittsburgh (sic.), Kan., and DeQueen, Ark., topping steep grades of the Ouachitas and Ozarks with such ease that one unit has since been removed." Note that the rendering shows two headlights, while they were actually delivered with single ones.

The First F3s

Electro-Motive Corporation had introduced the first four-motor freight cab unit, the 1350-h.p. model FT, in November 1939 and built more than 500 each cab and booster units during the war. In July 1945 EMD cleaned up the design as the 1500-h.p. F3, which quickly became its standard postwar production unit.

The production schedule at La Grange finally caught up to the KCS orders in late 1946, and the "five 6000-h.p. freight locomotives" from the August press release began to arrive in January 1947. The first freight F3s, two A-B-B-A sets numbered KCS 50ABCD and 51ABCD, were outshopped on January 10 and

EMC's FT DEMONSTRATOR 103, introduced in November 1939, was the first successful four-motor freight diesel. On its 50th anniversary (above), **one of the actual 103 cab units was on display at La Grange in September 1989. The styling on the 103 was the inspiration for the** *Southern Belle* **"bow wave" nose and side stripes.**

January 13, 1947, respectively. The units were classic three-porthole F3s, each powered by a 1500-h.p. EMD 16-cylinder 567B engine. They had single headlights, and the cab units had m.u. on the rear end only, with no nose receptacles.

6000 H.P. DIESEL LOCOMOTIVE . . DESIGNED AND BUILT BY ELECTRO-MOTIVE DIVISION . . GENERAL MOTORS . . LA GRANGE, ILLINOIS, U. S. A.

The remaining three sets followed four months later. The KCS 52ABCD-54ABCD were out-shopped between May 9 and 20, 1947. The EMDs wore the same "reversed" *Belle* livery that had been applied to the Erie Builts.

Passenger F3s

The final units mentioned in the August 17, 1946, press release were "two 3000-h.p. diesel-electric passenger locomotives," which were A-B sets of F3s. The KCS 30AB and 31AB were

THE 54A was rendered by EMD Styling Section artist Ben Dedek to publicize the KCS F3s (opposite bottom)**. A similar rendering was done for the passenger units** (right)**, clearly showing the upsweep on the B-unit. The 31A was at the old Rampart Street Station** (top) **in April 1951 with the** *Southern Belle*. **While the freight F3s had black side panels, the passenger F3s were delivered in the** *Belle* **green used on E-units.**

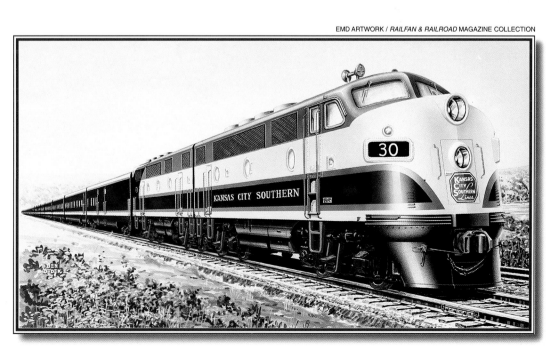

outshopped on November 12, 1947, with dual headlights and the full yellow-nose *Southern Belle* colors. Like the E-units, the boosters had the upsweep at the rear so that the two-unit set transitioned into the passenger cars the same way the E-units did. While the Erie Builts and freight F3 were delivered with black side panels, the passenger F3s retained the *Belle* green that had been introduced in June 1940.

Although the EMD Styling Section rendering (**page 45**) shows the three-porthole carbody, the two cab units were actually built with a revised center panel with four rectangular air filter grilles replacing the center porthole. Interestingly, the booster units retained the three-porthole layout.

JIM BOYD

Two L&A Erie Builts

Just a month after the arrival of the KCS 52-54 F3 sets, and before the November delivery of the passenger F3s, the Louisiana & Arkansas took delivery of two Erie Built cab units on June 23, 1947. The L&A 62A and 62C were purchased as freight units in the red livery with single headlights, but they were both fitted with train heat boilers for passenger service.

Fairbanks-Morse changed the styling on the Erie Builts in the spring of 1947, and the L&A units got taller and more upwardly curved windshields, compared to the squinty-eyed "Boeing B17" look of the earlier units.

THE EMD F3s had a long and productive service life. As intended in November 1947, F3A 31 was heading up No.15 (above) at Cedar Grove Yard in Shreveport on August 30, 1954 in the economy "Deramus red" livery. The lead unit of the second A-B-B-A freight set, the former 51A (opposite bottom) was easing a freight past the Shreveport Union Station in March 1968 in the late-1950s "blonde" paint scheme that was the first attempt to simplify the complex and expensive *Southern Belle* livery. The two Erie Built cab units, 62A and 62C, built for the L&A in May 1947, had upwardly curved windshields (opposite top), compared to the "squinty" ones that were on the six cabs delivered in November 1946 and January 1947, as shown (top) on the original 60A at Sheffield Tower in Kansas City in August 1966. The maintenance-prone FM opposed-piston engines were replaced by EMD 1750-h.p. 16-567C engines in the mid-1950s. The L&A 62A (opposite top) was at EMD in La Grange as KCS 62A after being repowered in May 1956.

More Freight F3s

The KCS and L&A were fully committed to dieselization and very happy with their EMD F3s and were putting orders for more units on the books as quickly as financing could be arranged. Following delivery of the passenger F3s in November 1947, in March 1948 the L&A received four A-B-B-A sets of freight F3s (55-58ABCD). Like the passenger F3s, they had the two-porthole and four filter grille side panels.

JIM BOYD

Oddballs and NW2s

Following the freight F3s of March 1948, in April the L&A picked up a lone Erie Built booster unit, 62B, to create an A-B-A freight set with the 62A and 62C. This brought the Erie Built fleet to three A-B-A sets, 60-62ABC.

In April 1948 the KCS received ten more NW2 switchers, 1212-1221, that were identical to the previous dozen.

In early 1948 EMD was working to improve the reliability of the F3 with beefed-up traction motors and generators. Electrical improvements included automatic transition (on earlier units, the engineer had to throttle down to "shift gears" by rearranging the connections between the main generator and traction motors). In March 1948 EMD built an "F5" testbed, 951,

that was an F3 with some of the electrical upgrades. The KCS bought the unit for a bargain price on October 28, 1948, and put it to work as L&A 59A. It was unique on the system in that it had the smoothly curved "passenger pilot" instead of the more stubby freight pilot.

Introducing the F7

With the dazzling Southern Belle livery, it's not surprising that EMD would arrange to debut its new F7 on the KCS order for two A-B sets of 1500-h.p. passenger units. The F7 incorporated a number of improvements that had been tested on the aforementioned F5, and an exterior that was impressively "cleaned up" with Farr air intake grilles.

The honor of being the "first F7" fell to L&A

KCS 1953 ANNUAL REPORT

THE EMD ARTWORK of the F3s (page 45) was used in advertising for "The NEW *Southern Belle*." This full page ad (above) was in the July 1949 *Trains* magazine.

A DOZEN EMD NW2s (1212-1221) were delivered to the KCS in May and June 1948. The 1214 was working the yard (opposite top) at Neosho, Mo., in May 1968. The EMD publicity photos of its first F7s show the black panels (above) on the 32A and the "transition" upsweep (below) on the 32B. The 1953 KCS *Annual Report* had artwork (opposite bottom) that apparently pre-dated the delivery of the 32, as it shows F7 32 and F3 53 with *Belle* green panels instead of black.

32A, which was outshopped by La Grange on February 17, 1949, along with booster 32B and cab 33A. Although they were photographed in the La Grange plant and delivered as an A-B-A set, they were intended to operate as A-B pairs, since the booster retained the upsweep at the rear to match the passenger equipment. The second B-unit, L&A 33B, was delivered eight months later on October 19, 1949.

As mentioned in the August 17, 1946, press release, the KCS had also ordered a number of new streamlined cars from Pullman and ACF to upgrade the passenger trains and actually expand the service. Between the delivery of the passenger F3s in November 1947 and the completion of the F7s in February 1949, the KCS had decided to change the *Belle* green on all the passenger cars and locomotives to a solid glossy black. The 32 set was the first to wear the new look.

Passenger Road Switchers

In early 1949, with big orders already on the books for more EMD F-units, the L&A had a need for a versatile locomotive that could do both passenger and freight work on a tight turn-around schedule. That was the literal definition of a road switcher, but EMD had no suitable unit in its catalog at the time, and the railroad was not about to venture into Baldwins or Alcos for just two units.

Since it already had nine Fairbanks-Morse units already on the roster, the system saw the FM H15-44 road switcher as a viable option.

The L&A 40 and 41, were delivered on May 21, 1949, equipped with steam boilers and decked out in the full *Southern Belle* passenger livery. The two units would work a cycle that would cover the New Orleans to Shreveport leg of the *Flying Crow* and the Shreveport-Hope *Shreveporter*, with layovers for freight work at Hope and Shreveport. With 100% availability, this would have been an amazing example of road switcher utilization.

FAIRBANKS MORSE H15-44s 40 and 41 arrived in May 1949 and were assigned to passenger duty on the L&A. The 41 was in full passenger colors (opposite bottom) at Shreveport in 1950. It was put into KCS freight service and painted black in 1952 and repowered by EMD in 1958. The repowered 41 (below) was at Decatur, Ark., on January 3, 1963, still wearing its inductive trainphone antenna. Dieselization was completed with the delivery of 15 cab and 19 booster freight F7s between November 1949 and March 1951. L&A 74A was in original colors at Kansas City (left) on September 7, 1959, in the company of Erie Builts.

THE FIRST FREIGHT F7 SET on the KCS was the A-B-A 70ABC. Lead unit 70A was still in the 1950s "blonde" scheme at Shreveport on May 25, 1977. In the late 1940s, the KCS could never quite figure out how to handle mixed unit numbers in one power consist. They adopted a system that permitted the crew to post the number of any unit in the consist in the indicator boards, but it soon deteriorated into an arbitrary and random assigning of numbers. The A-B-B-B "58" set (below) at Loring Lake, La., on February 8, 1955, wears an F3 number, although the only F3 in the set is a B-unit. The "116C" was southbound out of Texarkana in 1954 (right) displaying the number of a leased Chicago Great Western FP7! The CGW 116C was heading up an A-B-B-B-B-A "mortgage lifter" road set (opposite) at Oelwein, Iowa, in February 1965.

The FM's were set up for long-hood-forward operation. Their 8-cylinder opposed-piston engines, however, were plagued by the same bugs that beset the Erie Builts, and with the arrival of the four E8s in 1952 they were moved to the KCS at Pittsburg for local freight service.

In April 1958 the 41 was sent to EMD at La Grange and repowered with a 1750-h.p. 16-567C

engine – the same as the repowered Erie Builts! It was renumbered 45 and painted white in 1967. The 40 was retired in 1963 without being repowered.

Freight F7s

The KCS got EMD's first F7 in the form of passenger L&A 32A in February 1949. The KCS got the first of its A-B-A freight sets, 70ABC and 71ABC, in October of that year. In August 1950 these F7s were followed by the A-B-B-A KCS 72ABCD and 73ABCD and the A-B-B L&A 74ABC and KCS 59DBC (the latter to go with F5 59A) and boosters 75BC. The total fleet of 15 cabs and 19 boosters was rounded out in February and April 1951 with a scramble of L&A cabs 74D, 75AD and 76AD, plus boosters 76BC, 77BC, 78BC and 79B.

None of the KCS or L&A F7s were built

JIM BOYD

with dynamic brakes or nose m.u. receptacles (though many were later fitted with nose m.u.). All the freight units were outshopped in the "reverse" red *Belle* livery, and all the cabs had single headlights and were fitted with the inductive trainphone antennas.

The delivery of the final F7s in April 1951 effectively dieselized the KCS, although the last steam straggled into 1954.

COMING OUT OF the war, Bill Deramus made an important decision to modernize his trains and go aggressively after the passenger business. The wartime timetable had the *Southern Belle* on a 22-hour schedule between Kansas City and New Orleans, with its night run south of Shreveport. The *Flying Crow* between Kansas City and Port Arthur was on the opposite schedule, running at night on the north end. The *Crow* also had a daytime connecting section between Shreveport and New Orleans.

Along with the new streamlined cars from Pullman and ACF that were delivered in 1948, on April 3, 1949, the "new" *Southern Belle* was put into service on an 18-hour schedule, with its 10:00 a.m. departure from Kansas City set back to 4:00 in the afternoon, with arrival

The "New" *Southern Belle* of 1949

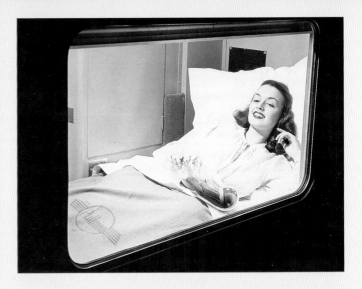

EIGHT 14-ROOMETTE, 4-DOUBLE BEDROOM sleepers were built for the L&A by Pullman in 1948. The *William Buchanan* was on the northbound *Southern Belle* (top) at Texarkana in March 1968. A "belle" was lowering the bed (above left) and posing beneath the Pullman blanket (above right) in a roomette – the photographer had to shoot from outside!

in New Orleans only two hours later, from 7:55 to 10:00 the next morning. The northbound *Belle* had the identical schedule. A connecting train from Shreveport carried the *Southern Belle* name into Port Arthur for the first time.

A third train, the nameless Numbers 9 and 10, were put on what was essentially the original *Southern Belle* schedule with the 10:10 a.m. to 7:00 a.m. run between Kansas City and New Orleans. This gave the KCS/L&A three trains each way a day between Kansas City and New Orleans and two each way a day between Shreveport and Port Arthur. The L&A *Shreveporter* was also

THE TWO ACF DINERS had stainless steel kitchens (above) and a 36-seat dining area (left) that was divided into three groupings of angled four-person and side-parallel two-person tables. The 59, *Old Plantation*, was on the *Southern Belle* at Texarkana (below) in May 1968.

retained between Hope and Shreveport.

The F3s and F7s were intended to help the prewar E-units in covering the expanded service. The streamlined passenger cars acquired in 1948 and 1949 included two mail-baggage-express (67-68), six coaches

(239-244) and two diners (58 *Mountain Lodge* and 59 *Old Plantation*) from ACF, and eight 14-roomette, 4-double bedroom sleepers from Pullman. The sleepers, named for past system presidents, were the *William Buchanan*, *Harvey Couch*, *William Edenborn*, *Job Edson*, *Stuart Knott*, *Colonel Fordyce*, *Leonor Loree* and *Arthur Stilwell*.

The coaches (60-seat chair cars) had oversize tinted windows and "Sleepy Hollow" reclining

THE OFFICIAL GUIDE OF THE RAILWAYS – NOVEMBER 1951

KANSAS CITY SOUTHERN LINES
K. C. S. Ry. — L. & A. Ry.
THE OFFICIAL GUIDE OF THE RAILWAYS – NOVEMBER 1951

Table 1—KANSAS CITY-NEW ORLEANS.

No. 15	1	9	Mls.	January 20, 1952.	No. 16	2	10
*9 30 PM	*4 00 PM	*9 30 AM	....	+..Kansas City, Mo.	7 45 AM	10 15 AM	7 45 PM
a –			22.5	....Grandview, Mo.	a –		
b –			37.8	.......Cleveland v	b –		
b –			47.2	........Lisle.. v	b –		
b –			52.3	+.....Drexel.. v	6 30		
b –			57.6	....Merwin.. v	b –		
b –			61.5	...Amsterdam.. v	b –		
b –			68.1	.....Amoret.. v	b –		
– –			74.0	......Tiger.. v	– –		
11 15			79.8	......Hume.. v	b –		
b –			88.2	..Stotesbury.. v	b –		
b –			92.8	....Richards.. v	b –		
b –			117.3	+..Mulberry, Kan.-Mo.	b –		
12 30 AM	6 15	12 10	128.4	+..Pittsburg, Kan.	4 55 AM	7 55	5 15
1 20	6 46	12 55	153.4	+..Joplin, Mo.	4 10	7 17	4 30
2 05	7 12	1 35	173.1	+..Neosho..	3 25	6 48	3 55
f2 15	f7 21	f1 45	179.5	....McElhany	f3 01	f6 39	f3 38
				(Camp Crowder) See Note▲			
f2 20	– –	– –	183.6	..Goodman, Mo. v	f2 56	– –	– –
f2 30	– –	– –	190.7	....Anderson.. v	f2 46	– –	– –
f2 40	– –	– –	194.1	....Lanagan.. v	f2 40	– –	– –
f2 50	– –	f2 09	199.6	......Noel.. v	2 30	– –	f3 10
f2 56	– –	– –	204.3	+..Sulphur Springs, Ark.. v	f2 24	– –	– –
f3 05	– –	– –	208.9	+.....Gravette.. v	f2 18	– –	– –
f3 15	– –	– –	216.0	....Decatur.. v	f2 07	– –	– –
f3 23	– –	– –	221.4	....Gentry.. v	f2 00	– –	– –
3 35	8 22	2 50	228.3	+..Siloam Springs v	1 50	5 42	2 32
f3 45	– –	– –	234.9	....Watts, Okla.. v	f1 35	– –	– –
f3 55	p	– –	243.4	...Westville.. v	f1 21	– –	p
f4 12	p	– –	257.2	....Stilwell.. v	f1 01	– –	p
d –	– –	– –	270.6	......Bunch.. v	d –	– –	– –
d –	– –	– –	280.1	...MarbleCity.. v	d –	– –	– –
5 05 AM	9 34	4 10	290.2	arr....Sallisaw ..lve.	12 13 AM	4 32	1 15
v5 55 AM	v10 20	v5 00	327.4	arr...Fort Smith, Ark..lve.	v11 20 PM	v3 40	v12 20
v3 40 AM	v8 40	v3 15	327.4	lve.+.Ft. Smith, Ark..arr.	v1 00 AM	v5 55	v2 05
5 05 AM	9 34	4 10	290.2	lve.+..Sallisaw, Okla...arr.	12 13 AM	4 32	1 15
2 –	– –	– –	306.8	.....Redland.. v	2 –	– –	– –
5 45	h9 56	4 45	310.7	+......Spiro... v	11 45 PM	h4 08	12 48
2 –	– –	– –	316.4	.....Panama.. v	d –	– –	– –
6 10	h10 13	5 05	324.4	+......Poteau.. v	11 15	h3 50	12 25
f6 20	h10 21	f5 13	331.4	+......Howe.. v	f11 05	h3 43	f12 17
6 40	10 30	5 25	337.1	+....Heavener.. v	10 55	3 37	12 10
f7 02	– –	– –	353.8	......Page.. v	f10 16	– –	– –
7 40	:11 20	6 25	378.8	+....Mena, Ark. v	9 43	:2 45	11 10
7 55	– –	– –	391.3	...Hatfield, Ark.. v	f9 23	– –	– –
f8 01	– –	– –	395.9	......Cove.. v	f9 17	– –	– –
f8 07	– –	– –	400.8	...Vandervoort.. v	f9 11	– –	– –
f8 16	– –	– –	407.8	....Wickes.. v	f9 02	– –	– –
f8 31	– –	– –	420.3	....Gillham.. v	f8 47	– –	– –
9 00	12 35	7 40	432.4	+....De Queen.. v	8 30	1 35	10 00
9 13 AM	– –	– –	442.0	arr...Neal Springs.. lve.	8 06 PM	– –	e –
9 35 AM	– –	e –	443.3	arr..Horatio, Ark.(Bus.)lve.	*7 45 PM	– –	e –
8 50 AM	– –	e –	443.3	lve..Horatio, Ark.(Bus.)arr.	8 30 PM	– –	e –
9 13 AM	– –	e –	442.0	lve..Neal Springs, Ark.arr.	8 06 PM	– –	e –
f9 21	– –	– –	448.4	....Winthrop.. v	f7 59	– –	– –
f9 29	– –	– –	455.1	......Allene.. v	f7 46	– –	– –
f9 38	– –	– –	461.9	......Wilton.. v	f7 37	– –	– –
9 46	– –	f8 21	466.9	+.....Ashdown.. v	7 32	– –	f9 13
10 15	1 36	8 50	486.9	arr.+.Texarkana, Ark.-Tex.lve.	7 05	12 25	8 45
10 35	1 40	9 05	486.9	lve..Texarkana, Ark.-Tex.arr.	6 50	12 20	8 30
11 03	– –	– –	507.5	....Bloomburg.. v	6 20	– –	– –
11 16	– –	– –	519.6	...Rodessa, La.. v	6 06	– –	– –
11 28	– –	f9 57	527.0	+.....Vivian.. v	5 57	– –	f7 43
f11 33	– –	– –	536.0	.....Oil City.. v	f5 44	– –	– –
f11 43 AM	– –	– –	539.6	..Mooringsport.. v	f5 39	– –	– –
12 20 PM	3 00	10 45	560.1	ar.+.Shreveport.. v	*5 10 PM	11 00	7 00
				(Union Station)			
....	3 15	11 25	0	lve.+.Shreveport, La.....arr.	....	10 45	6 25
....	4 14	– –	44.9	+...Coushatta.. v	....	9 39	– –
....	f4 42	– –	69.1	+....Clarence.. v	....	f9 11	– –
....	5 13	– –	97.8	+.....Colfax.. v	....	8 40	– –
....	....	12 26	30.2	lve.+..Minden, La..lve.	....	....	5 27
....	– –	– –	35.1	.....Sibley.. v	....	– –	– –
....	– –	– –	50.0	...Jamestown.. v	....	– –	– –
....	– –	f1 02	57.0	.....Castor.. v	....	– –	f4 46
....	– –	– –	81.7	....Goldonna.. v	....	– –	– –
....	– –	1 56	99.8	+....Winnfield.. v	....	– –	3 47
....	– –	– –	125.8	....Dry Prong.. v	....	– –	– –
....	5 50	3 15	122.4	+..Alexandria, La.. v	....	8 10	2 32
....	– –	– –	141.0	......Bijou.. v	....	– –	– –
....	– –	– –	146.1	.....Hessmer.. v	....	– –	– –
....	f6 27	3 55	153.4	.....Mansura.. v	....	f7 30	1 37
....	– –	– –	157.8	...Moreauville.. v	....	– –	– –
....	– –	– –	168.6	...Simmesport.. v	....	– –	– –
....	8 15	5 58	233.7	+..Baton Rouge.. v	....	5 45	11 40
....	f8 42	– –	255.1	.....Gonzales.. v	....	f5 14	f10 50
....	– –	f6 56	285.7	....La Place.. v	....	– –	f10 15
....	– –	– –	302.0	......Norco.. v	....	– –	f10 07
....	9 53	7 31	310.3	....Carrollton Ave..	....	4 10	9 41

Table 2.
KANSAS CITY-SABINE DISTRICT.

No. 3	1-101	Mls.	January 20, 1952.	No. 4	102-2
....	*4 00 PM	0	+..Kansas City, Mo.	....	10 15 AM
....	6 15	128.4	+...Pittsburg, Kan.	....	7 55
....	6 46	153.4	+....Joplin, Mo.	....	7 17
....	7 12	173.1	+....Neosho v	....	6 48
....	v8 40	327.4	lve.+.Ft. Smith, Ark...arr.	....	v5 55
....	:11 20 PM	378.8	+......Mena.. v	....	:2 45
....	12 35 AM	432.4	+...De Queen.. v	....	1 35
....	1 40	486.9	+.Texarkana, Ark.-Tex.	....	12 25 AM
....	....	519.6	⊙...Rodessa, La..	....	....
....	....	527.0	+.....Vivian.. v	....	....
....	3 00 AM	560.1	ar.+.Shreveport.. v	....	*11 00 PM
			(Union Station)		
*9 30 AM	3 30 AM	560.1	lve..Shreveport, La...arr.	4 40 PM	10 10 PM
f10 04	– –	579.1	+....Frierson.. v	f4 03	– –
f10 09	– –	583.0	+...Kingston.. v	f3 58	– –
10 25	f4 25	594.1	+...Mansfield.. v	3 45	f9 12
f10 43	– –	607.0	+.....Benson.. v	f3 27	– –
f10 51	f4 51	612.9	+...Converse.. v	f3 20	f8 46
f10 59	– –	619.3	+.....Noble.. v	f3 13	– –
11 08	f5 06	624.5	+.....Zwolle.. v	3 08	f8 32
f11 26	5 23	641.6	+......Many.. v	2 51	8 16
f11 33	f5 33	641.8	+.....Fisher.. v	f2 41	f8 06
f11 38	f5 38	645.2	⊙....Florien.. v	f2 33	f8 01
f11 52 AM	f5 52	654.9	+...Hornbeck.. v	f2 20	f7 48
f12 01 PM	f6 03	661.3	+...Anacoco.. v	f2 10	f7 38
12 25	6 25 AM	671.2	+...Leesville.. v	1 55	7 25 PM
f12 45	– –	686.3	...Rose Pine, La.. v	f1 30	– –
1 00	6 53	691.7	+...De Ridder.. v	1 24	655
f1 24	f7 17	707.3	+.....Singer.. v	f1 03	f634
1 40 PM	7 40 AM	721.7	arr..+.DeQuincy, La...lve.	12 45 PM	6 15 PM
f3 00 PM	f9 00 AM	744.0	arr....Lake Charles, La....	*11 15 AM	f4 45 PM
1 40 PM	7 40 AM	721.7	lve...De Quincy, La...arr.	12 45 PM	6 15 PM
f2 02	f8 03	737.8	+.....Starks.. v	f12 23	f5 51
f2 09	– –	743.1	+....Ruliff, Tex.. v	f12 15	– –
f2 20	f8 22	752.7	+..Mauriceville.. v	f12 03 PM	f5 33
2 55	8 47	769.0	arr.+.Beaumont.. v	11 35 AM	5 10
2 55	8 52	769.0	lve..Beaumont.. v	11 35	5 10
f3 10	– –	778.6	+...Nederland.. v	f11 06	– –
3 30 PM	9 30 AM	786.6	+...Port Arthur.. v	*10 50 AM	*4 30 PM

EXPLANATION OF SIGNS.

*Daily.

a Trains will stop on flag to pick up or discharge revenue passengers to and from Pittsburg or beyond.

b Trains will stop on flag to pick up or discharge revenue passengers to or from Kansas City or beyond and to and from Pittsburg or beyond.

c Trains will stop on flag for revenue passengers to or from Shreveport or beyond when advance request is made to agent.

d Trains will stop on flag to pick up or discharge revenue passengers to or from Siloam Springs and beyond and to and from Heavener or beyond.

e Trains will stop on flag to pick up or to discharge revenue passengers to or from Spiro or beyond and to or from Texarkana or beyond, with tickets from or to Horatio, Ark.

f Flag stop to pick up or discharge revenue passengers.

h Trains will stop on flag to pick up or discharge revenue passengers to or from Joplin and beyond and to or from Texarkana and beyond.

p Trains will stop on flag to pick up or discharge revenue passengers to or from Neosho or beyond and to or from Spiro or beyond.

i Daily bus service between Lake Charles and De Quincy.

v Daily bus service to and from Fort Smith.

x Trains will stop on flag to pick up or discharge revenue passengers to or from Kansas City or beyond.

: Trains will stop on flag to pick up or discharge revenue passengers to or from stations that are regular stops.

△ Non-agency stations.

⊙ Telephone stations.

+ Coupon stations.

Note ▲—Bus between McElhany (Camp Crowder) and Neosho to and from all regularly operated Frisco trains.

STANDARD—*Central time.*

56

seats. Although the term Jim Crow was never mentioned, this was the Deep South in the 1940s, and segregation was a way of life. Two of the six chair cars were "divided coaches." All of the coaches carried names, with the divided cars being the *Texarkana* and *Kansas City* and the undivided being the *Shreveport, Alexandria, Baton Rouge* and *New Orleans*.

Included in the order from ACF were the two new diners, *Old Plantation* and *Mountain*

KANSAS CITY SOUTHERN LINES
K. C. S. Ry. — L. & A. Ry.
THE OFFICIAL GUIDE OF THE RAILWAYS – NOVEMBER 1951

Table 3.
HOPE, MINDEN AND SHREVEPORT.

	No. 3	Mls.	*January 20, 1952.*		No. 4	
			LEAVE|ARRIVE			
	*4 30 A M	0	Hope		8 10 P M	
	f 4 47	11.4	+ Patmos		f 7 50 "	
	5 04	23.1	+ Stamps		7 35 "	
	f 5 13	29.3	McKamie		f 7 27 "	
	f 5 19	33.6	Experiment		f 7 21 "	
	f 5 29	41.4	+ Taylor		7 12 "	
	5 40	48.0	+ Spring Hill		7 04 "	
	f 5 52	55.7	Sarepta		f 6 49 "	
	6 02	61.2	+ Cotton Valley		6 42 "	
	6 34	78.5	arr. + Minden lve.		6 12 "	
	6 34	78.5	lve. Minden arr.		6 12 "	
	f 6 56	92.5	Princeton		f 5 46 "	
	7 30 A M	108.2	arr. + Shreveport lve.		*5 10 P M	

The Shreveporter

(Union Station.)

Table 4.
HOPE-MINDEN-ALEXANDRIA-NEW ORLEANS.

	Mls.	*October 1, 1950.*	
	0	+ Hope	
	23.1	+ Stamps	
	78.5	+ Minden	
	147.8	+ Winnfield	
	194.3	+ Alexandria	
	384.6	+ New Orleans	

EQUIPMENT.

Trains 1 and 2— *Southern Belle*
Streamlined—Air-Conditioned—Diesel Powered.
Chair Cars between Kansas City-New Orleans and Port Arthur.
Diner—Between Kansas City-New Orleans and Port Arthur.
Tavern-Lounge-Observation — Between Kansas City-New Orleans (bar service in Missouri and Louisiana).
Sleepers—Between Kansas City and New Orleans (Cars 1 and 2) 14 Roomette, 4 Double Bedrooms; between Kansas City and Port Arthur (Cars 3 and 4) 14 Roomette, 4 Double Bedrooms.

Trains 3 and 4— "*The Shreveporter*"
Air-Conditioned—Diesel Powered.
Chair Cars between Hope and Port Arthur.
Cafe-Coach-Lounge between Hope and Port Arthur.
Sleeper St. Louis to Shreveport—14 Roomette, 4 Double Bedroom (17). (On Missouri Pacific No. 31 to Hope, Louisiana and Arkansas No. 3 to Shreveport) (northbound via Texarkana).

Trains 9 and 10.
Streamlined—Air-Conditioned—Diesel Powered.
Chair Cars—Between Kansas City and New Orleans.
Diner-Lounge—Between Kansas City and New Orleans. (Bar service in Missouri and Louisiana.)
Sleepers—Between Kansas City and New Orleans (Cars 9 and 10) 10 Section, 3 Double Bedrooms; between Shreveport and New Orleans (Cars 109 and 110) 14 Roomette, 4 Double Bedrooms. (May be occupied at 9 30 p.m. and until 8 00 a.m.)

Trains 15 and 16— The *FLYING CROW*
Air-Conditioned—Diesel Powered.
Chair Cars—Between Kansas City and Shreveport.
Sleepers—From Shreveport to St. Louis. 14 Roomette—4 Double Bedrooms (323.) (On Train 16 to Texarkana, Missouri Pacific No. 32 to St. Louis) (southbound via Hope).

Trains 101 and 102.
Streamlined—Air-Conditioned—Diesel Powered.
Chair Cars—Between Kansas City and Port Arthur.
Cafe-Coach-Lounge—Between Shreveport and Port Arthur.
Sleeper between Kansas City and Port Arthur—14 Roomette, 4 Double Bedrooms.

EXPLANATION OF SIGNS.
* Daily.
† Daily, except Sunday.
f Flag stop to pick up or discharge revenue passengers.
∆ Non-agency stations
⊙ Telephone stations.
+ Coupon stations.
STANDARD—*Central time.*
🚗 Rail-Auto Service available at this point.

Table 5.
SHREVEPORT AND DALLAS.

	Mls.	STATIONS.		
	0	Shreveport		
	20.9	Lorraine		
	22.2	Waskom		
	49.3	Jefferson		
Freight	76.4	Hughes Springs	Freight	
Service	82.7	Daingerfield	Service	
only.	98.4	Pittsburg	only.	
	108.5	Newsome		
	117.8	Winnsboro		
	140.4	Sulphur Springs		
	171.5	Greenville		
	185.2	Farmersville		
	224.5	Dallas		

Table 6.
ARKANSAS WESTERN RAILWAY.

	No. 3	Mls.	STATIONS		No. 4	
			LEAVE ARRIVE			
Irregular.		0	+ Heavener, Okla.			Irregular.
		13.5	⊙ Bates, Ark. ∆			
		19.0	⊙ Cauthron, Ark. ∆			
		21.2	⊙ Oliver ∆			
		25.8	⊙ Hon " ∆			
		31.8	arr. ⊙ Waldron " lve.			
		55.8	arr. Forester " lve.			

Table 7.
FORT SMITH AND VAN BUREN RAILWAY.
Coal Creek, Okla., to West Panther Okla. (20 miles). Freight service only.

Coupons of One-Way or Round-Trip Tickets Calling for Passage—

1. Between Little Rock or beyond and Shreveport or beyond via MoPac Hope L&A, or MoPac Texarkana T&P, or MoPac Texarkana KCS will be honored via Hope L&A, or Texarkana KCS.
2. Between St. Louis or beyond and Alexandria or beyond via MoPac will be honored via Hope L&A, or Texarkana KCS Shreveport L&A.
3. Between Shreveport or beyond and Alexandria or New Orleans or beyond routed L&A or T&P will be honored by either line.
4. Between KCS stations north of Texarkana and Houston or beyond via Texarkana T&P Longview Junc. IGN, or Shreveport SoUPac, or Beaumont GCL, or Beaumont SoUPac will be honored via any of the four routes named.
5. Between Shreveport or beyond and New Orleans or beyond via L&A will be honored via L&A Baton Rouge Teche Greyhound Lines.
6. Between Kansas City, Mo., and Joplin, Mo., via KCS or MoPac will be honored via either line (applies only on tickets reading to or from Joplin).
7. Between Shreveport or points beyond and Alexandria to Baton Rouge via L&A will be honored via T&P to or from Addis. Passengers to make own arrangements between Baton Rouge and Addis.
8. Between Shreveport or points beyond and Alexandria to Addis, La., via T&P will be honored between Baton Rouge and Alexandria or Shreveport or points beyond, via L&A on payment of: Adult Ticket $0.78 first class, $0.82 coach class; Half-Fare Tickets $0.39 first class, $0.41 coach class. Passengers to make own arrangements between Addis and Baton Rouge.

The optional routes are also good in the reverse direction.
Note—Coach multi-ride commutation tickets will be honored under item 5 only.

Eureka Springs, Ark. — Rail Service to and from Siloam Springs.

57

SIX ACF CHAIR CARS of 1948 featured Heywood-Wakefield "Sleepy Hollow" seats (below) that were "scientifically designed for full comfort" as the result of a Harvard University study of 3867 posteriors. Big windows gave the cars a bright interior (left). When the new *Belle* was placed on a faster schedule, its old timetable slot was filled with new Numbers 9 and 10. Number 9 (opposite top) was traversing the 63rd Street Viaduct in Kansas City on July 7, 1952.

JIM BOYD

JIM NEUBAUER

Lodge, that featured three grouped dining areas with angled four-seat tables opposite two-seat tables parallel to the wall. Total seating capacity was 36. The large kitchens were all stainless steel for cleanliness and ease of maintenance and included Stearnes propane gas ranges, steam cookers, steam tables and Surgex electric dishwashers.

Two of the Pullman-built tavern-observation cars from the 1940 *Southern Belle,* the *Kansas City* and *Shreveport,* were rebuilt by ACF in 1948 as the 54 *Good Cheer* and 55 *Hospitality.* These cars boasted that "... the

TWO 1940 Pullman tavern-obs cars were rebuilt in 1948 for grill service as the *Hospitality* (above), at the Smoky Hill Museum in Lenexa, Kan., in July 1971, and *Good Cheer* (above left), stored at Shreveport in March 1968.

Western Electric Program System is compactly panel-built near the bar, and appropriate radio and wire-recorded music will be heard throughout the train. Individual speakers are located in each room of the sleeping cars."

Two mail-baggage-dormitory cars were included in the 1949 delivery, and they served an important function. U.S. Mail contracts were lucrative business, checked baggage had to be handled, and express packages were also a big business for the railroads in these pre-FedEx days. And Bill Deramus was not about to deface his shiny new streamliners with heavyweight head-end cars.

The ACF steel cars, 67 and 68, rode on four-wheel trucks and had toilets, wardrobes, refrigerators and steam cookers for the Post Office employees, while the dormitory sections provided the dining car crew with toilets, showers, berths and closets.

COMPARE THE OBS SECTIONS between the 1940 (above) and 1948 (right) configurations. The cars were rebuilt from tavern-lounge to provide a small grill dining section to permit them to replace the full diner on Trains 15 and 16.

THE LAST PREWAR E3, No.23 was on the northbound *Southern Belle* (above) at Mooringsport, La., on March 31, 1946. On August 10, 1951, the unit was wrecked and sent to EMD at La Grange to be "rebuilt" as an E8m, emerging in January 1951, still carrying its number. The road-weary E8m was on the southbound No.15 (below) at Texarkana in April 1968. The rebuilt unit carried a stubby "freight" pilot, as did E9m 25 (right).

SHORTLY AFTER THE REBUILT 23 was sent home from La Grange, the KCS took delivery of four new E8s, 26-29, between January 31 and February 8, 1952. The first of the new E8s, the 26 (opposite bottom) was on the southbound

Southern Belle at De Queen, Ark., in October 1965. The E6 No.25 was selected for rebuilding at La Grange and emerged in June 1959 as an E9m. The rebuilt 25 was on the southbound No.15 (opposite top) at Texarkana in March 1968.

1952: The E8s Arrive

ANY DOUBTS ABOUT Bill Deramus' commitment to passenger service were swept away on January 31, 1952, when the KCS began taking delivery of four new 2250-h.p. E8 cab units from EMD. The 26-29 would release the more versatile passenger F3s and F7s for freight service, since the KCS had concluded that the 2000-h.p. E-units were the ideal power packages for its typically modest-sized streamliners. The boiler-equipped F-unit cabs and boosters would still be available if needed.

The new E8s carried the full *Southern Belle* livery and had the elegantly curved "passenger

JIM BOYD

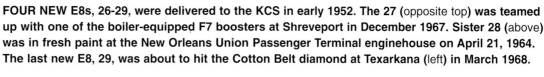

FOUR NEW E8s, 26-29, were delivered to the KCS in early 1952. The 27 (opposite top) was teamed up with one of the boiler-equipped F7 boosters at Shreveport in December 1967. Sister 28 (above) was in fresh paint at the New Orleans Union Passenger Terminal enginehouse on April 21, 1964. The last new E8, 29, was about to hit the Cotton Belt diamond at Texarkana (left) in March 1968.

pilots." Like the F-units, however, they had no dynamic brakes or nose m.u. receptacles (although nose m.u. was later applied). The stainless steel Farr radiator grilles were panted red, but the paint quickly wore off, and the appearance of the units varied over the years as the grilles turned silver and got repainted and weathered again.

A Different Slant

On August 10, 1951, slant-nosed E3 23 had a severe head-on collision with a troop train at Lettsworth, La. It was sent to EMD at La Grange where its trucks and main generators were salvaged and "rebuilt" as an E8. The new 23 was actually an "E8m," derated to 2000-h.p. out of deference to the older electrical gear. It was returned to the KCS in January 1952, just a few days before the four new 2250-h.p. E8s began to arrive.

A similar situation took place in early 1959 when E6 25 was returned to La Grange and rebuilt as a 2000-h.p. E9m. Both the rebuilt 23 and 25 were essentially identical to the new E8s, except that they were fitted with the stubby "freight" pilots. ⊚

Switchers and Geeps

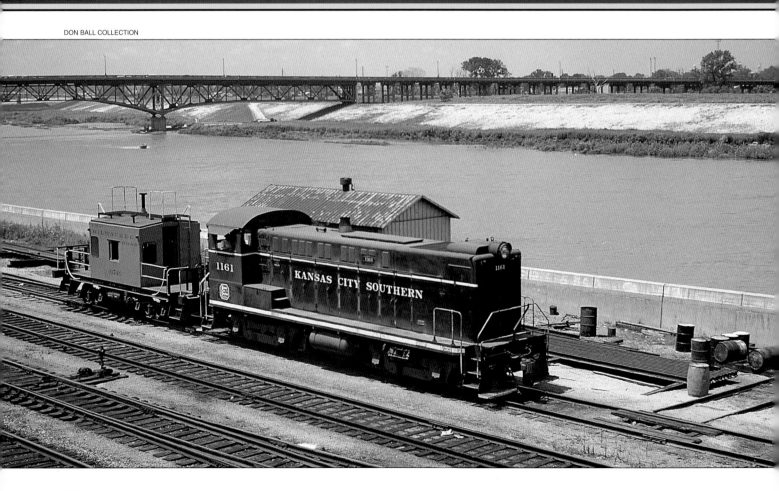

THE SW7 REPLACED THE NW2 in EMD's catalog in late 1949, and in the winter of 1950-'51 the KCS/L&A got 16 of them (1300-1315). SW7 1308 and NW2 1214 were on the Knoche turntable (opposite top) in August 1971. Baldwin

S12s 1160 and 1163 (above) were working Knoche Yard in May 1968, while 1161 (opposite bottom) had a Joint Agency Milwaukee Road caboose hop along the Kaw River in August 1958 after delivering to the Santa Fe's Argentine Yard.

O N THE SAME DAY that EMD outshopped the first A-B-A set of freight F7s for the KCS, it also delivered five more NW2 switchers (1222-1226). The date was October 19, 1948, and one year later EMD replaced the 1000-h.p. NW2 in its catalog with the 1200-h.p. SW7. Both were powered by the 12-cylinder 567A engine, and the most noticeable external change was a much larger radiator in the nose in front of single belt-driven fan, rather than the two smaller fans in the NW2.

The KCS was still using 0-8-0s in Kansas City in 1950 when it ordered 16 of the new SW7s. The KCS 1300-1309 were outshopped in late October 1950, with the L&A 1310-1315 following in January 1951. These units differed from the NW2s in that they were equipped

for multiple-unit operation and fitted with end walkover platforms. The KCS and L&A assigned the SW7s where the m.u. could come in handy on road locals in combination with yard duties. The standard black switcher livery with white stripes prevailed.

Back to Baldwin

The little Baldwin VO660 of 1946 (**page 43**) must have made a reasonably good impression on the KCS, because it was in Kansas City in 1950 when Baldwin sent its new 1200-h.p. S12 demonstrator there and went back to Eddystone with an order for four new units.

In April 1951 the KCS took delivery at Kansas City of four Baldwin S12 switchers. Although on the books as L&A 1160-1163, the

quartet went to work in Kansas City and stayed there for their entire careers, never once reaching L&A "home rails!"

The Baldwins were stripped-down models, with air-actuated throttles and no m.u. The beefy Westinghouse generator and traction motors should have made them great luggers, but the S12s were relative lightweights (at 109 tons, they were 14 tons less than the NW2s)

and got a reputation for being slippery, under-powered and prone to electrical problems. In spite of this, they survived until 1968.

How Do You Use a Geep?

In October 1949 EMD's Dick Dilworth put the streamlined dandy F7 into work clothes and created the 1500-h.p. "General Purpose" GP7 road switcher. The Alco RS1 of 1941 was

STEAM WAS STILL WORKING the Kansas City Joint Agency transfer runs while the KCS was getting its Baldwin S12s and EMD SW7s and GP7s. The L&A's ex-FEC 0-8-0 251 (opposite bottom) was on the road on February 1, 1953. Baldwin S12 1163 (below), outshopped on April 13, 1951, was working Knoche Yard on April 24, 1967. The KCS Lines' first GP7, L&A 150, had a transfer (left) at West Wye Tower bound for Argentine Yard on March 25, 1967. The Illinois Central's first GP7, 8950, built a year before KCS 150, wore the same basic EMD livery (above) at Mendota, Ill., on February 9, 1964.

the first true road switcher, and by 1947 Alco, Baldwin and FM were all marketing 1500-h.p. road switchers. In reality, EMD came in last with the best.

The KCS sampled five GP7s (L&A 150-154) in November 1951, but its "cab-and-booster mentality" kept the KCS and L&A from fully appreciating the versatility and potential of the Geep. The L&A units had m.u. but no dynamic brakes, and their basic black switcher livery gave a strong indication of how management regarded the units. Though occasionally paired, as the RS1s had been, they were generally assigned singly to yard jobs and dodgers, and it would be years before they were considered anything more than just "big switchers."

1953: A Few More Geeps

THE KANSAS CITY SOUTHERN got its first five GP7s (L&A 150-154) in November 1951 and followed up a little more than a year later in February 1953 with eight more, L&A 155 and KCS 156-162. They were identical to the previous Geeps and went into similar yard and local service. It was rare to see them working in road sets with the F-units or in consists of more than two Geeps together.

Following the February 1953 delivery of the GP7s, the KCS bought no new road power for more than six years, when it got three GP9s in June 1959! While roads like the Illinois Central were making wholesale commitments to road switchers, the KCS continued to lash up its cabs and boosters. It would be many years and a change of management before the KCS would abandon its commitment to F-units. 🚂

THE FIRST GP7 in the February 1953 delivery was L&A 155, which was working Kansas City (above) in May 1968. The 156 was the first of the seven Geeps for the KCS proper. In a vision that would have been a horror to Bill Deramus in 1953, the northbound *Southern Belle* was departing Texarkana (opposite top) with the 156 leading an E8. More typical of Geep assignments was the 161 working a "dodger" local at Zwolle, La., (opposite bottom) on February 17, 1955. In June 1959 the KCS picked up its final three high-nosed Geeps in the form of GP9s 163-165. The "middle" unit of that set, 164, was working in New Orleans (below) in August 1968. All the KCS and L&A Geeps operated short-hood forward.

T**HE ANHEUSER-BUSCH COMPANY** operated the Manufacturers Railway in St. Louis to serve its breweries, and it had a reputation for spit 'n' polish appearance and maintenance. When it put three 1000-h.p. Alco high hood switchers up for sale in early 1956, the KCS sensed a bargain. Since it already rostered four RS1s powered by the same 539 engine, the KCS was not venturing into unknown territory. The 539 was a rugged chunk of cast iron that was so overbuilt that it was virtually indestructible. The high hood carbody equipment layout was "backwards," with the engine and generator up front and the radiator next to the cab instead of at the front of the hood.

The Manufacturers 201-203 were 1000-h.p. units, powered by the turbocharged 539 engine and riding on the simple but rugged Blunt trucks. They had been built in February 1940 and maintained in excellent condition. The KCS purchased them directly in April 1956 and put them right to work, still in green and gold, as L&A 1121-1123.

While they were at it, the KCS picked up another bargain high hood from the Toppins Machinery Company of Pittsburg, Kansas. It was a 900-h.p. unit that had been built in October 1937 as Youngstown & Northern 211, and it became L&A 1120 on April 16, 1956. It went to the Kansas & Missouri subsidiary that operated eleven miles of trackage on the Kansas side of the Kaw River in Kansas City. It was sold to K.C. Public Service Co. in 1964.

The former-Manufacturers units generally stayed in the Kansas City terminal area, but in the mid-1960s the 1122 was assigned to the yard job at DeQueen, Ark., that had been the final home of the lone Baldwin VO660. The 1121 and 1123 were traded to EMD in 1966, and the 1122 followed in September 1968.

New High-Hood Alcos in 1956?

THE FORMER MANUFACTURERS RAILWAY high hood Alco switchers were bought in April 1956 and put in more than a decade of service on the KCS, even though they were on the roster as L&A units. The 1123 (left) looked well-maintained at Kansas City on the Fourth of July, 1961. The 1122 was at the Shreveport shop (above) on April 27, 1968, before returning to the yard assignment at DeQueen, Ark., where is was resting (below) three months later in July. The 1122 was traded to EMD in September 1968.

JIM BOYD

EMD ARTWORK / THREE PHOTOS by JIM BOYD at La GRANGE, SEPTEMBER 1967

Birth of the Blondes

THESE UNDATED RENDERINGS by Styling Section artist Ben Dedek show proposals for simplifying the *Southern Belle* freight livery that was used on the F3s. They clearly show F7s, but all the KCS units were factory painted in the full red *Belle* livery. These appear to be EMD "after market" suggestions for the KCS to use in its home shop repaints, the first of which were the Erie Builts that were sent to La Grange in 1955 for repowering (pages 48 and 53). Pioneer F3 51 (right) was in the adopted "blonde" livery (left) at Shreveport in March 1968, and F7 75 (below) was there in March 1975. The 91, built as 74D, was at Pittsburg (opposite bottom) in May 1971.

THE FINAL NEW FREIGHT cab units delivered to the KCS were the F7s of April 1951, and they were factory painted in the full reverse red Southern Belle livery. When it came time to do the first repaints at the Pittsburg shop, however, the KCS took a serious look at simplifying the freight scheme.

The repowering of the FM Erie Builts in early 1955 seems to have prompted the change. Part of the deal was that the KCS would overhaul and paint the units before they were shipped to La Grange.

A series of renderings by Styling Section artist Ben Dedek (**opposite top**) appears to show EMD offering options for simplified striping that included what became the "blonde" scheme applied by the KCS to the EMD-bound Eries (**page 46**) and subsequent freight repaints.

CHAPTER 4

THE EIGHT GP7s that arrived in February 1953 completed the initial dieselization of the KCS and L&A, and the last steam was retired in mid-1954. With the expense of new motive power now behind him, Bill Deramus turned his attention to the operational mess in Shreveport that had been a leftover from combining the KCS, LR&N and L&A. The railroad had two separate yards, two passenger stations and a number of industrial switching

ABOVE / JIM BOYD

TOP PHOTO / WARREN CAILEFF

areas in the city, and chaos usually prevailed.

Plans were drawn up for a new yard along the KCS main line northwest of downtown Shreveport, about halfway to Blanchard. The $6.5 million project included a large diesel shop and a huge car shop. It was opened in April 1956 and named "Deramus Yard" by order of the board of directors. A new 17-mile line off the west end of the yard created a new connection to the Texas line.

By the mid-1950s, the KCS and L&A were

settling down to business as a modern and prosperous railroad, and only one piece of operational nonsense remained to be resolved. The 91-unit fleet of cabs and boosters still carried their A/B/C/D number designations, and the dispatchers and train crews were still rather randomly assigning numbers to multiple-unit road sets (**page 55**). It was not uncommon for the same engine numbers to show up on two different trains on the same dispatcher's trainsheet (proving that Dilbert was reality

THE NEXT BIG PROJECT following dieselization was the construction of the new Deramus Yard and diesel shop at Shreveport, where blonde F3 51 (opposite) was moving out in March 1968. Bill Deramus was succeeded as president in 1961 by his son, William N. Deramus III. A father-and-son portrait (below) was made in the 1940s. The first "second generation" power for the KCS was ten GP30s in May 1962, three of which were at Shreveport (above) on May 10, 1968.

A New Generation

long before computers came along). On January 1, 1957, a superintendent's bulletin was put out that renumbered all the "control units" (**pages 40-41**), finally ending the confusion.

Bill the Third

William Neal Deramus, president of the KCS in 1957, was actually a "Junior." His father was William Neal De Ramus, but after the son simplified the spelling of his family name to Deramus, he never used the "Junior" as part of his name. His brother Louis, who was the president of the Chicago, Indianapolis & Louisville (the Monon) from 1938 to 1946, kept the De Ramus spelling. When Bill Deramus' son was born on December 10, 1915, following the family tradition,

he was named William Neal Deramus III.

Young Bill went to the University of Michigan and Harvard Law School and began railroading on the Wabash in 1939. During the war, he ran the railroads in India as a Major in the U.S. Army Transportation Corps. He returned home in 1946 to a position as assistant general manager on the KCS. Two years later he became president of the struggling Chicago Great Western at the age of 33.

It's not surprising that the CGW had the same devotion to cab-and-booster F-units and long trains as the KCS, since father and son were dieselizing their respective railroads at the same time.

The economies of the diesel helped Deramus put the CGW back on its feet, and his aggressive style of management won him the respect of the industry,

though his methods and military style were not always popular among the employees.

On January 8, 1957, Bill Deramus III left the CGW to take over as president of the seriously ailing Missouri-Kansas-Texas, that had already dieselized and was still in deep trouble. He went right to work cutting costs wherever possible and trying to get the physical plant back into shape. Passenger service was an obvious target, and he cut back without killing it completely.

He literally "left his mark" on the railroad by adopting the spartan "Deramus red" paint scheme with nothing to relieve the solid color but small gold Katy heralds on the sides and nose. Even in his absence, the Chicago Great Western followed suit by changing its simplified solid purple livery to Deramus red.

Developing the Dynasty

While Bill Deramus III was coping with the Katy, his 75-year-old father's health was beginning to deteriorate. On November 2, 1961, the younger Deramus left the Katy to assume the presidency of the KCS, while his father retained his post as chairman of the board.

Deramus Red GP30s

The order for ten GP30s was already on the books when son Bill took over as president of the KCS in early 1962, but the units were delivered in the solid red livery he'd instituted on the Katy. The 100-109 were the first units on the KCS, to be equipped with dynamic brakes.

The ten GP30s were purchased outright with trade-ins, but a significant change in the tax laws for 1962 permitted depreciation of in July 1963. Interestingly, the two groups of GP30s were not identical, since between the orders EMD had extended the left side of the cab back about a foot to make more room inside for the head brakeman's seat.

During the 1950s the operating philosophy on both the KCS and CGW had been to run long freights with as many cars as possible to reduce the number of train movements and crews. Trains of 200 or more cars with six F-units

UNDER WILLIAM NEAL DERAMUS III the Katy adopted the spartan "Deramus red," with the small herald, as shown on E8 54A (right) at Kansas City Union Station with Rock Island E6 630 in 1963. John W. Barriger III, who succeeded Deramus a few years later, brightened up the image with the traditional red and white Katy herald, as shown on EMD-repowered Alco FA1 83C (below) at Parsons, Kan., in May 1968. When he became president of the KCS, Bill Deramus acquired the railroad's first turbocharged and low-nosed "second generation" diesels, GP30s 100-109, in May 1962. Ten more (110-119) followed in July 1963.

KANSAS CITY SOUTHERN GP30 112 (opposite top) was at Shreveport on September 11, 1970, in its factory red and black. The only number painted on it is a tiny numeral above the fuel tank. The Chicago Great Western got 201-208 in the mid-1963 in nearly identical Deramus red livery. The 207 (opposite bottom) was eastbound at Byron, Ill., in 1964.

equipment in 15 years instead of 20, and that would encourage trade-ins over rebuilding or repowering of oddball units like the FM's (or in the Katy's case, Baldwins and Alcos). An order was soon placed for ten more GP30s, and the first F-units to be retired were used as trade-ins. GP30s 110-119 were outshopped were not uncommon, and four GP30s yielded the same horsepower. Long trains were not forgiving of rough handling, however, and the GP30s had a bad habit of wheel-slipping and lurching, tearing the trains apart. As a result, the KCS was not interested in the GP30's successor in the EMD catalog, the GP35.

"Second Generation" E7s

WHILE WILLIAM N. DERAMUS III had severely cut passenger service on the Katy, he surprised nearly everyone by adopting his father's pride in the KCS passenger trains. Under the senior Deramus, the third main line trains (Nos. 9 and 10) were dropped north of Shreveport in 1958, but the rest of the service not only remained intact but was being constantly improved. The trains were heavily advertised, and low fares promoted a

MAINE CENTRAL E7 709 (opposite) was at Augusta, Maine, on No.14, the southbound *Pine Tree*, in September 1952. In November 1962 it became KCS 20 and was on No.16 at Shreveport (above) on July 7, 1966. MEC 705 became L&A 6 a year later. It was at New Orleans (below) on June 12, 1965. Note the different number boards and windows/portholes.

high level of coach ridership and Pullman occupancy. The program of rebuilding and upgrading the streamlined cars, begun right after the war, was an ongoing project.

While two of the prewar E3s and E6s had been rebuilt, the remaining three were nearing the end of their economic life. Meanwhile, up in Maine, the Maine Central was getting out

of the passenger business and put a group of E7s up for sale. In September 1962 the KCS purchased MEC 709 and brought it home to become KCS 20, swapping its MEC maroon for the full *Southern Belle* livery. A year later the KCS bought four more of the MEC E7s, and in November 1963 MEC 705-708 became L&A 6 and KCS 7, 11 and 12 (assigned by filling

JIM NEUBAUER

KANSAS CITY SOUTHERN E7 No.7, on the *Southern Belle* (above) south of Kansas City in April 1966, was built as Maine Central 706, shown (opposite top) arriving at St. John, New Brunswick, with the *Gull* on July 20, 1956. The 1946 E7s had the small number boards and the MEC's earlier green livery, compared to the 1948-built 709 (page 78) in

B&M maroon. Note the similarity of the EMD Styling Section paint schemes on both MEC and KCS units. KCS 11 (MEC 707) and 7 were crossing the Highway 50 viaduct south of Kansas City (opposite bottom) with the *Southern Belle* in June 1967, while KCS 12 (MEC 708, with portholes like the 6, was at Texarkana (top right) on Train 15-9 in April 1968.

in some "blanks" in the original number system without duplicating timetable train numbers). It's difficult to think of 1946 E7s as "second generation" power, but they permitted KCS to retire the last of its slant-noses shortly thereafter.

Maine Central 705-708 had been built in June 1948, while the 709 (KCS 20) had come along

in July 1948. The most noticeable "factory" difference is that the 709 had the newer large number boards, but the 705 (L&A 6) and 708 (KCS 12) had been modified with portholes in place of the carbody side windows. All the E7s had single headlights, while the 12 and 20 were later fitted with nose m.u. by the KCS. ◉

FORMER-NEW YORK CENTRAL observation- lounge 42 was at Texarkana in 1963 (above) before it was reconfigured into a grill-lounge-obs for food service on trains that didn't carry a full diner. After rebuilding it was painted into the black *Belle* livery that it was wearing (below) in March 1968.

The 270-series Pullman coaches of 1965 (opposite top and bottom right) had comfortable but Spartan interiors. Those ten cars permitted retirement in 1966 of the four 1937-built Osgood-Bradley "American Flyer" coaches, that were still stored in Kansas City (opposite bottom left) in July 1970.

New Passenger Cars in the 1960s

THE KCS PASSENGER DEPARTMENT was constantly seeking ways to improve service and equipment. In 1956 it bought five new 260-series economy coaches from ACF and got ten new baggage-express cars from Pullman in 1959.

In 1960 it purchased four New York Central 1948 Budd stainless steel observation-lounge cars. The KCS reconfigured these as grill-lounge-observations to provide food service. In 1965 it picked up two more of the NYC cars, bringing the obs fleet to six and permitting retirement of the Hospitality and Good Cheer.

The former-NYC cars worked for the first few years in pure stainless with just a black letterboard, but beginning in 1964 they were painted into the black Belle livery. The paint didn't adhere very well to the stainless, and the cars required constant maintenance.

As remarkable as it seems, the KCS went back to Pullman in 1965 for ten new 270-series easy-to-maintain economy coaches. At a time when other railroads were killing theirs, the KCS was still improving its streamliners.

SD40s and White Paint

IF THERE WAS EVER a locomotive designed with the KCS in mind, it was EMD's SD40. Ever since Bill Deramus discovered F-units and jumper cables, the operating philosophy of the KCS had been to run fewer trains with more cars.

The "longer/fewer" dream seemed to settle down at the 200-car range simply because of coupler strength and air brake performance. A six F-unit 9000-h.p. set could handle the long trains, and theoretically they could be replaced by four 2250-h.p. GP30s or three 3000-h.p. SD40s.

The key was "wheels on the rail," though, and the GP30s proved to be slippery and prone to lurching with their relatively primitive wheelslip system. EMD was very aware of this problem and made a big advance when it introduced its "1966 Line" (GP40, SD40 and SD45) with the new 645 engine, AC/DC electrical system and the revolutionary IDAC (Instantaneous Detection And Correction) wheelslip system.

Instead of completely dropping the load with a mechanical relay to stop the slip like the old DC systems, IDAC electrically sensed a pending slip and instantly but gently reduced generator excitation until the slip stopped – and just as quickly it smoothly restored the power, almost completely eliminating the lurching.

The KCS immediately placed an order for 14 of the new SD40s (600-

FOUR PHOTOS / JIM BOYD

THREE GHOSTLY SD40s were carrying the new KCS image into Texarkana (above) in April 1969. The 608 and 600 (opposite bottom) were heading up another set making a set-out and pick-up at Texarkana a week later. Note the tiny engine number on the side of the cab. Unseen in this view is a fourth radio-controlled SD40 two-thirds of the way back in the 200-car consist. The Locotrol console (right) in the cab of the 608 gives the engineer control of the "slave" 607, shown (below) leaving town.

613), and they rolled out in mid-October 1966 in a striking new solid white livery with a gold ScotchLite frame stripe, huge red KCS letters on the hood and miniscule road numbers on the side of the cab. All had dynamic brakes.

For the past few years the Southern Railway had been experimenting with radio-controlled mid-train "slave" units, and the KCS saw this as the solution to powering and breaking its mega-freights. The SD40s were ordered with Locotrol command consoles on four units (604, 605, 608 and 609) and remote receivers on four more (606, 607, 610 and 611). The remaining six units had no Locotrol equipment, and in the white paint, they added a whole new dimension to the term "plain vanilla."

The remote slaves were initially used as single units, but they could be m.u.d with non-radio units to create bigger mid-train sets. The slaves were positioned in the rear half of the train according to a tonnage formula and could be used both for power and dynamic braking.

One afternoon in Texarkana, a slave-damaged car into a siding from behind with the slave unit. On a subsequent encounter, the engineer told me that when he reported the incident, the trainmaster told him, "That was some pretty sharp railroading, but if you ever do it again, you're fired. We don't want people driving trains with nobody aboard!"

The King is Dead …

Unfortunately, Bill Deramus did not live to see his ultimate locomotives conquer his longest trains. The elder Deramus was chairman of the board of KCS Industries when he died on December 2, 1965, while his son continued as president of the railroad.

SW1500s and White Paint

One month after the SD40s arrived, the KCS received its first new switchers since the SW7s of 1951. As part of the 1966 Line, EMD had created the SW1500, powered by the 1500-h.p. 12-cylinder 645 engine. The KCS took delivery of SW1500s 1500-1503 in November 1966 in the white paint. These were followed up with

JIM BOYD

equipped train tore out a drawbar about halfway between the lead units and the slave. The damaged coupler was on the "wrong" end (facing the road power) and could not be coupled onto to be set out. The engineer simply isolated his road units and used the radio to shove the

1504-1517 and SD40s 614-621 in August 1968.

By the fall of 1966, all locomotives being overhauled and painted at Pittsburg were emerging in the white livery. This included a number of veteran F3s and F7s that were being upgraded to F7 and F9 specifications.

JIM BOYD

THE SOLID WHITE LIVERY that was introduced with SD40 600 on October 13, 1966, was thereafter made standard and applied to all subsequent repaints. The SD40s had dynamic brakes and could m.u. effectively with the GP30s, as shown at the Texarkana Trigg Street Yard (opposite bottom) in March 1968 alongside NW2 1222. The first SW1500s (1500-1503) were delivered only a month after the SD40s. The 1505 (below), part of the August 1968 group (1504-1517) was photographed in 1970. The first F-unit to get the white was L&A 95, shown (above) in April 1968 at Hope, Ark., fresh from the Pittsburg paint shop and renumbering. It was the only unit to get the red stripe. The 58A had been upgraded to F7 specs in 1953. In February 1967 the KCS leased its only "conventional" Alco switcher from Precision National. The former Kansas City Terminal 1940-built Alco S2 No.51 was painted white as KCS 1114. It was working Kansas City (right) in October 1968. Before it suffered an engine failure and was returned to PNC in June 1971, it had become the last Alco on the KCS.

DAVID CASH

MAC OWEN / MATT HERSON COLLECTION

CHAPTER 5

BETWEEN THE PURCHASE of the red GP30s in 1963 and the end of passenger service on November 2, 1969, the KCS went through its most colorful years. The only livery missing from the roster during this period was the original reverse red *Belle* freight livery, but it was supplanted by the Deramus red and the new white of 1966.

This chapter explores the images of the KCS of that time, beginning at Kansas City Union Station and terminating in New Orleans. Both first and second generation diesels were working side by side in this last colorful era.

ON A DREARY MARCH 25, 1967, ex-MEC E7s 7 and 12 and a passenger F7B (below) were easing out of the west end of the Kansas City Union Station trainsheds after bringing Train 10-16 in from New Orleans and Port Arthur.

MATT HERSON

The Last Colorful Decade

SOUTHERN BELLE No.1 was rolling east from Union Station on a bright morning in August 1968 (above) with E8 28 and another F7B, toward Sheffield Tower, where it would turn south to depart the city. On the south side of Kansas City, E7 No.6 had No.1 making track speed (below) in May 1968 with two of the 1964 Pullman-built economy baggage cars.

"A RATTLER ON THE HAYWIRE" is how the operator at Sheffield Tower in Kansas City described the approaching northbound freight headed by the EMD-repowered Erie Built 61A in August 1965. It was trailed by two F7Bs, and Erie B and Erie cab 60A (page 49). The Fairbanks-Morse builders plate (left) is off the 61A.

THE POWER SET from the "rattler" tied up at the Joint Agency engine terminal at the old KCS East Kansas City Yard, know now as Knoche Yard. The 61A (above) was sandwitched between Milwaukee Road U25B 389 and S4 switcher 811. The 60A showed its majestic size (below) at the other end of the set. In spite of their size, the big Eries were now essentially "just F-units" with 1750-h.p. EMD 16-567 engines. Unlike the rebuilds of the Katy Alco FA1s (page 81) that got new EMD radiators and cooling fans in a rooftop hump, the Erie rebuilds kept their original radiators.

THE 1112, THE ONLY KCS RED RS1, (opposite bottom), was working the yard alongside the 60A. The KCS had acquired the unfortunate nickname, "the Haywire," during the steam era, as a result of its unconventional operating practices – like using compound 0-6-6-0s as road engines – and the name just wouldn't go away. The Joint Agency yard and roundhouse on the northeast side of Kansas City, south of the Missouri River, was the focal point for interchange and transfer operations, although the KCS had other smaller yards in the greater Kansas City terminal district.

THE JOINT AGENCY engine terminal (above) had Erie Built 64 showing faint traces of its blonde livery in July 1964 as it headed up a set of F7s, with a Milwaukee Road F7 set behind it. In a tradition typical of the late 1960s (page 64), Milwaukee MP15 443 (left) had a white KCS transfer caboose in Kansas City on February 26, 1979. A remarkable match of liveries had occurred (below) on July 11, 1953, when new E8 28 got paired up with one of the 1947 F3B's, still in passenger yellow, on the northbound *Southern Belle* on the 63rd Street Viaduct at Swope Park between Grandview and Kansas City.

PITTSBURG, KANSAS, 128 miles south of Kansas City, is the home of the KCS' biggest locomotive backshop. In July 1962, Erie Built 63 (above) was resting outside the main shop building. In May 1968 the dead line behind the shop (top) included veteran E7s 20 and 11 and passenger F3 31. Four months later all three were traded to EMD. Meanwhile, at the passenger station, (right) fresh E7 6 was ready to swap off with the inbound unit on No.2, the northbound *Southern Belle*. On May 11, 1968, K.C.-Port Arthur Trains 15/16 and Shreveport-New Orleans 9/10 were discontinued, leaving only *Southern Belles* 1 and 2.

JIM BOYD

JIM BOYD

DAVID CASH

THE BUSINESS CAR *TOLMAK* **was built in 1966 – yes, 1966! – by Darby of Kansas City. Named for Texas, Oklahoma, Louisiana, Missouri, Arkansas and Kansas, it was in Texarkana** (above) **on No.1 in April 1968. The "senior" business car was the** *Kay See*, **built by Pullman in 1928 and upgraded at Pittsburg in 1950. It was in Kansas City** (above right) **in August 1966 and with new stainless railings** (right) **at Joplin in July 1969.**

SOUTHBOUND *SOUTHERN BELLE* No.1 was making the station stop at Siloam Springs, Ark., in April 1969 (opposite top **and** above) with a tavern-obs replacing the full diner since the discontinuance of Nos. 15-9 and 16-10 in May 1968.

Number 1 was at Joplin Union Station (top) in late May 1968 with passenger F7 32 and E7 6 for power. The 32 lost its lower headlight when its nose door was swapped out. On the rear of this *Belle* was the heavyweight business car *Tolmak*.

FAIRBANKS-MORSE REPOWERED H15-44 No.45 spent most of the 1960s working the Pittsburg-Watts Dodger and the Baxter Springs Branch Dodger, even though it was officially an L&A unit. It was in fresh white paint (below) laying over at Watts, Okla., in May 1968, and with black Geep 161 and an E8 (above) at Pittsburg in February 1969. Its non-repowered sister 40 had been scrapped in 1964, but the 45 functioned as a GP9-in-strange-clothes until 1971.

ERIE BUILT 64A had an impressive road set (two F3B's, two F7B's and an Erie B and trailing Erie cab) at Poteau, Okla, (above) on April 9, 1966. Interestingly, the compact H15-44 (opposite) packed the same EMD power plant as the huge Erie Builts, both producing 1750-h.p. from a 16-567C. The repowered Eries were all traded to EMD in late 1966.

"Science Fiction" Cabooses

BETWEEN THE SPACE ALIEN marker lights on the roof and the bizarre Rockwell LFM trucks, the 42 stainless steel cabooses (302-344) built by the Darby Corporation between 1964 and 1970 were stunningly futuristic. The 300 (above right), at Memphis in November 1969, built by Morrison International in 1963, was KCS' first bay window buggy. "Science Fiction" cabooses 305 (above left) and 328 (below) were crossing the Cotton Belt main line and T&P Paris branch diamonds at Texarkana in 1968 and 1976, respectively.

PAGE, OKLAHOMA, is a brief "sag" in the middle of the 32-mile 1.5% climb south from Heavener, Okla., to Rich Mountain, Arkansas. Late one afternoon in May 1968, a northbound freight with three SD40s, led by the 601, met a southbound Dodger (above) with GP9 165 at Page. The road job pulled up with a set-out that was plucked off (opposite top) from behind the SD40s by the Geep. After putting the cars behind the caboose, the Geep ran around to the north end of its consist in the pocket and cleared up the passing track for the approaching *Southern Belle* while the freight got its train back together on the main. Number 1 rounded the curve (below) at the north passing track switch.

THE SOUTHBOUND *BELLE* eased into the passing track (above) and passed through (above right) between the freight and the Dodger (demonstrating precisely where that "Dodger' name came from). A soon as the CTC switch lined and the signal cleared, the freight moved out (right) to clear the south switch to let the *Belle* back onto the main.

DeQUEEN, ARKANSAS, 433 miles south of Kansas City, was the division point between the Fourth and Fifth Subdivisions. By July 1968 it wasn't quite the important place that it had been in the steam era (the turn-around point for the 2-10-4s, for example, which could not be used south of there because of some trestles), but it was still a crew change point. In the evening light, *Southern Belle* No.1 was rolling through the yard (above), alongside the DeQueen & Eastern interchange yard. It pulled down to the passenger station (below), where a fresh engine crew took over (right). By now the *Belle* was the only remaining KCS passenger train, and the grill-tavern-obs has replaced the full diner. The yard work at DeQueen was light enough that the KCS assigned its last high hood Alco, 1122, that spent most of its time (opposite bottom left) parked near the freight yard.

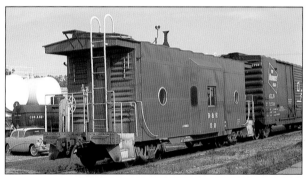

THE DeQUEEN & EASTERN and Texas, Oklahoma & Eastern were owned by the Dierks Forest Company and reached 40 miles in each direction east and west out of DeQueen, where they interchanged with the KCS. D&E D6 (right) was a GP35, bought new in 1964. Caboose 80 (above right) was obviously one of the buggies built by the KCS from boxcars at the Pittsburg Shop during the 1940s and modernized with sheathing and portholes.

THE RED RIVER swamplands above Texarkana are traversed by a series of timber trestles. In July 1968 I drove out to photograph the northbound *Southern Belle* No.2 and saw this bridge from Highway 59. Train time was close, so I trotted across a cornfield to set up the shot. I was surprised – and a bit disappointed at the time – to see the A-B-A set of F-units ahead of the E8. So much for a perfect "portrait" of the *Belle*. The obs was a nice touch, though. I headed back toward the car and noticed that the furrows between cornrows were moving. They were full of *snakes*! Dozens of 'em! I made that last 100 yards to the car in giant strides hitting only the tops of the rows. And now you know the *rest* of the story.

THREE PHOTOS / JIM BOYD

THE TEXAS-ARKANSAS STATE LINE cuts down the main street of Texarkana and right through the front door of Union Station's north facade (opposite bottom inset). The KCS passes west of Union Station on the Texas side, and its passenger trains had to back in or out. In March 1968, E8 29 and an F3B (above) were bringing southbound 15-9 around the connection from the north-south KCS main in the background and into the platforms (opposite bottom) of Union Station. To depart, it would back out to the main and then head south. Freight F3 94 (54A) and an E7 (top left) had another 15-9 pulling into the platforms just a few days before it was discontinued on May 11, 1968. The conductor was "tail-hosing" the northbound *Southern Belle* No.2 (top right) backwards around the connection in March 1968.

SOUTHBOUND KCS TRAINS using Texarkana Union Station had to back westward out to the main line, as F3 94 was doing (left) on 15-9 in May 1968. The stairways made for interesting photography.

A SUDDEN "*BAMP!*" on the chime horns put the pigeons to flight as Blonde F7 91 and the unlettered L&A E7 No.6 pulled under the Viaduct Road bridge (above) with the southbound 15-9 in April 1968 and eased the train into the Union Station platforms (top). The open walkway over the platforms made Texarkana a grand place to just watch the trains. The "other" portholed E7, KCS 12, and an F7B had the northbound *Southern Belle* departing Texarkana (top left) that same month and was photographed from the Viaduct Road bridge that spanned the KCS connection and the Texas & Pacific and Cotton Belt main lines. The Missouri Pacific from Little Rock became Texas & Pacific at the Texarkana yard, which was south of Union Station and north of the Cotton Belt main line and freight yard.

TEXARKANA UNION STATION served the KCS, Missouri Pacific, Texas & Pacific and Cotton Belt in its heyday. The Cotton Belt ended passenger service in November 1959, but in the spring of 1968 the MoPac/T&P still had three trains in each direction, and two of each three were at night. The big *Texas Eagle* hit Texarkana at 2:50 in the morning westbound. The MoPac crew handed off their train to the T&P crew (opposite top) in May 1968. A month earlier, GP30 117 (below) had been teamed up with E8 27 at the same spot with a late-running northbound KCS 10-16. On a different night a few weeks earlier (opposite bottom), the grill-obs on 10-16 was awaiting departure. The crew of the southbound *Southern Belle* No.1 (above) stretched their legs during the 20-minute stop at 8:30 in the evening.

THE SOUTHBOUND 15-9 had a scheduled 20-minute stop in Texarkana, and in March 1968 its E8 and F3B had cut off at the east end of the station (above) to pick up an express car. It backed down on its train (opposite top) with the McCartney Hotel towering in the distance. Ticket agent Sidney Webb (top) was an employee of the Texarkana Union Station Company, while local railfan Noble Butler (top center left) was a frequent spectator. The Texarkana Model Railroad Club (top center right) occupied a large room in the southwest end of the station. In an insurrection, the HO gaugers had voted the O gaugers off the island and relaid their big 60-inch radius curves with double track HO.

A MID-TRAIN SLAVE SD40 was banging the Cotton Belt main line diamonds (below) as it rolled southward in April 1968. The Texas & Pacific main line to San Antonio crosses the Cotton Belt in front of the tower. For a view looking north on the KCS from the Cotton Belt, see page 70. The Cotton Belt has a main line fuel rack behind the photographer.

THE CAB-AND-BOOSTER F-UNIT TRADITION was alive and well on the KCS in the late 1960s. Red F7 89 (72D) had two F7B's, an F3B and a GP30 (above) southbound out of Texarkana in April 1968. Veteran passenger F7 33A of the original L&A 1947 A-B-A set (below), was decked out in the new white as it headed up a five-unit set at Kearnak, Texas, on March 14, 1971. Even as the KCS was trading in some F-units, others were being overhauled and upgraded.

THE TIMBER TRESTLE over an inlet of Caddo Lake at Mooringsport, La., (about halfway between Shreveport and Texarkana) carried the northbound *Southern Belle* No.2 on June 28, 1969, with E9m 25 (opposite bottom) on the front and business car *Tolmak* on the rear. A week later, on July 6, No.2 was in the care of E8 27 (opposite top), one of only two E-units (with E8m 23, page 118) to get the white paint. The *Southern Belles* lasted until November 2, 1969.

TILLIE CAILEFF

TWO PHOTOS / WARREN CAILEFF

SHREVEPORT UNION STATION was modernized in May 1940 (below) for the inauguration of the *Southern Belle*. At that time, the station served the Illinois Central, Texas & Pacific and Texas & New Orleans (SP), as well as the KCS. The L&A had its own Central Station that also served the Cotton Belt. Both moved into Union Station on May 26, 1940. One morning in March 1968 I had followed IC's Vicksburg passenger train 205 into Shreveport from Gibsland. It arrived (right) at 12:30 and pulled up west of the station beneath the Common Street bridge, as KCS E7 No.7 and an F3B idled by the platforms. The IC train pulled south and backed into the stub-end terminal. The train bulletin (below right) showed the line-up.

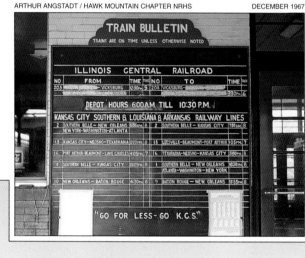

THE OLD *FLYING CROW*, Train 15-9 from Kansas City, arrived behind freight F7 93, E8 27 and an F7B shortly after the IC train came in. It backed into the platforms (above) from the Wye junction south of the station. Then NW2 1222 went to work to split it into No.9 for New Orleans and No.15 for Port Arthur. The F7 was cut off and backed past the E-units into a spur (opposite center). With its train reconfigured, No.9 departed behind E8 27 by pulling out and backing north (opposite bottom) to the "Horn Track" wye and over the SP's Red River bridge at Bossier City to the L&A line to New Orleans. Meanwhile, the IC train had been pulled out, turned, serviced and returned to the terminal.

THE SHREVEPORTER
TRAIN No. 15- 1:05 P.M.
TO
MANSFIELD LAKE CHARLES
MANY   BEAUMONT
LEESVILLE PORT ARTHUR

A PLATFORM SIGN dating to the Louisiana & Arkansas days (left) identified No.15 as the *Shreveporter*, though that name was no longer in use. It had the number, destinations and departure time correct, however. The E7 had been idling all day, and No.15 made a very smoky departure (above) directly south out of the station. A short while later a freight from the New Orleans line approached the Common Street bridge (below) on Lake Street alongside the Jefferson Hotel.

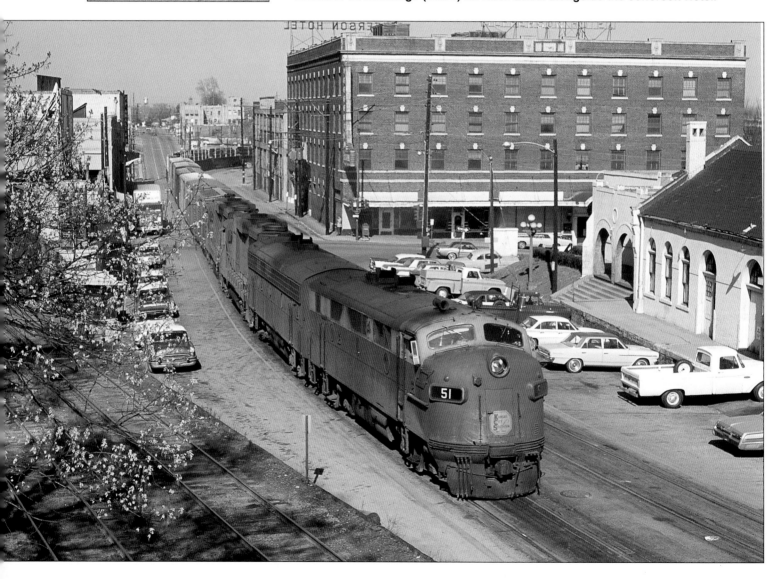

"BLONDE" F3 51 eased its train under the Common Street bridge (left) and pulled past the F-units idling at the passenger terminal. When the freight cleared, IC 208 backed out (above) for its 174-mile run to Vicksburg. The train had previously run 313 miles to Meridian, Mississippi. A leased Chicago Great Western mail car (below) was being used for materials storage at Shreveport.

HARRIET STREET YARD was one of the numerous small facilities that served the KCS and L&A before operations were consolidated at Deramus Yard, three miles west of there. On December 14, 1968, white GP30 109 and two red sisters (below) had freight 42 from New Orleans rolling under the Portland Street bridge and past the yard office.

ONE OF ONLY TWO WHITE E-UNITS, E8m 23 was ready to depart New Orleans at 10:00 p.m. with *Southern Belle* No.2 in August 1969, just three months before all passenger service on the KCS would end. By this time, one of the ex-NYC grill-obs cars (opposite bottom) had replaced the full diner on No.2. The L&A main line into New Orleans passed Rozal's Motel in Metairie (right) where white F7 89 and a GP30 were passing on August 17, 1969. The darkening sky was the approaching Hurricane Camille, that would hammer the area that night. The weather was much better in November 1967 (below) when veteran NW2 1201 in fresh Deramus red was working New Orleans West Yard.

ABOVE and TOP / JIM BOYD

ARTHUR ANGSTADT / HAWK MOUNTAIN CHAPTER NRHS

NEW ORLEANS UNION PASSENGER TERMINAL was opened on May 1, 1954, and the KCS moved in from the old L&A Rampart Street Station. The NOUPT stub-end station was worked by three EMD SW8s (left). KCS E7 No.6 and Illinois Central E8 4019 were at the LAUPT shop (above) in May 1964.

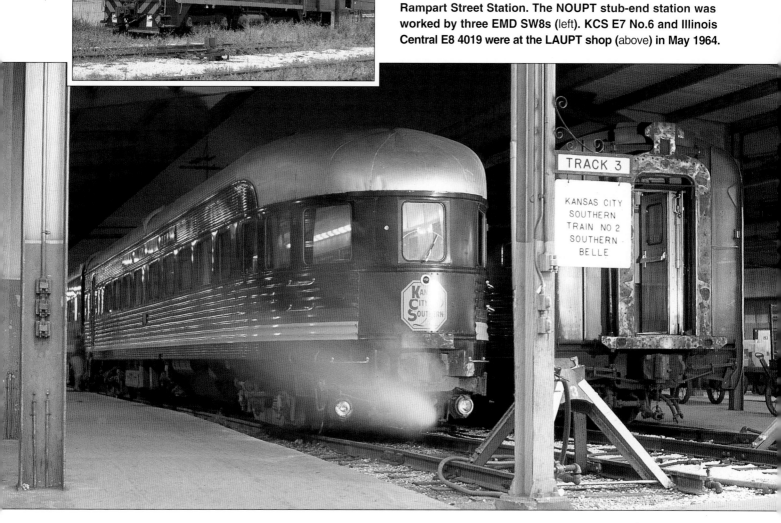

CHICAGO RAILFAN JIM NEUBAUER went to Kansas City in April 1968 to visit his friend Phil Weibler and took the opportunity to ride the *Southern Belle*. He left at 9:45 in the morning on No.1 and arrived at Noel, Mo., at 2:05 in the afternoon. After a one-hour wait, he caught No.2 back to K.C. E8 29 and a white F7B headed up No.1 at Kansas City (above and left). He shot the depot at Hume, Mo., (bottom left) from the back window of the ex-NYC cafe-obs and also photographed its interior (bottom right) looking toward the rear.

Round Trip: Kansas City to Noel

SOUTHERN BELLE No.1 sped southward, overtaking a freight (right) powered by a GP30 and red F7s and meeting a northbound freight with three SD40s (below center right) at what appears to be Joplin. Back in his seat, Jim used the end mirror (below left) to take a self portrait while photographing the coach interior. Somewhere south of Pittsburg, he used the Dutch door (bottom) to photograph the meet with the Watts-Pittsburg Dodger with EMD-repowered FM H15-44 No.45 that "owned" the job in the late 1960s.

THE STATION STOP AT NOEL was long enough for Jim to get up front (top) to photograph the train and its departure (above left) with UP and SP sleepers ahead of the obs. Between the 2:05 departure of No.1 and the 3:05 arrival of No.2 he snapped the Noel depot (right). The northbound *Southern Bell* came in (below) with GP30 100 ahead of the E8. Jim used the Dutch door (bottom right) to photograph the train curving through the Ozark hills. The trainman obviously had no problem with the open window riding.

CHAPTER 6

IN JANUARY 1969 the *Southern Belle* was northbound near Joplin and would not survive to see another winter. By now the cafe-obs had replaced the full diner, and the head-end business had dwindled, but the consist still included two coaches and a New Orleans-K.C. sleeper.

The Future Looks Gray

THE BEGINNING OF THE END for the era of "Streamlined Hospitality" came in 1967 when the U.S. Post Office Department began terminating its rail mail contracts. The RPOs and bulk mail handling contributed heavily to the KCS passenger revenues. The last RPO cars were removed on January 12, 1968, and as a result, the K.C.-Port Arthur Trains 15-9 and 10-16 (the remnants of the old *Flying Crow*) were discontinued on May 11, 1968. The K.C.-New Orleans *Southern Belle* rang on until November 2, 1969.

The *Southern Belle* discontinuance notice to KCS passengers over the signature of W.N. Deramus III, President, concluded: "We deeply regret the situation which brings about this action. (We, too, have loved the passenger train!)" To his credit, Deramus had run a clean, friendly and efficient passenger service right to the end. The timing of the discontinuance was fortunate, since the KCS was out of the picture when Amtrak was created in 1971, and Deramus was able to avoid that political chaos completely.

While the end of passenger service brought a dramatic visual change to the KCS with the loss of the colorful streamliners, an even deeper change had begun in 1962 when the senior Bill Deramus had become a pioneer in

rail corporate "diversification" by creating Kansas City Southern Industries to venture out into non-rail investments and management. Both father and son became heavily involved with the process and left the "hands-on" running of the railroad to others while the corporate officers utilized the railroad's income and equity as a "cash cow" for their other ventures.

When Deramus Senior died on December 2, 1965, Bill III moved up to KCSI chairman. He'd gained a reputation on the Great Western and Katy for "creating money" by cutting back on trackwork, and this "deferred maintenance" was being practiced on the KCS in the late 1960s. It caught up with him in December 1972 when a series of derailments began to tie up the railroad for weeks at the time. The wicked combination of poorly maintained track and long heavy trains in cold and wet winter weather had caused the railroad to literally

FOUR DISPLACED E-UNITS (29, 25, 27 and 23) were on the Cullen Turn (above) passing the vacant L&A shop buildings at Minden, La, on November 15, 1969. They worked freight for a few months before retirement. The fleet of cafe-obs cars (below) was gathered at Pittsburg on May 15, 1970.

collapse upon itself. And all of this at a time when traffic was booming from a massive grain export deal with the Soviet Union.

Bill Deramus III realized that a full-time

PAUL WALTERS

THE KCS KEPT BUYING six-motor EMDs, like SD40-2 668 (above) at La Grange in August 1976. The 688 (top), meeting a northbound at Page, Okla., in July 1982, was one of 16 long-nosed SD40-2s (677-692) built in 1978 and '80. GP40 759 (below) was Penn Central 3187, bought from Conrail in 1984. It was at Lamar Street in Dallas on April 18, 1984 with slug 4077, GP40-2 slug master 796 and ex-PC GP40 772. Two slug master F7A's, two F7B slugs and a Geep were on the "Tidewater Turn" coal train (opposite bottom) out of Sulphur Springs on January 29, 1984, at the electrified TUGCO power plant railroad interchange at Monticello, Texas.

railroader was needed to put his trains back on track, and he brought up vice president of operations and veteran civil engineer Thomas S. Carter as the railroad's president in 1973. In the era marked by the collapse of the Penn Central and Rock Island, it looked like the KCS would be the next in line. But Carter went to work and poured money into the track and roadbed and got the KCS ready for the heavy unit trains from the Montana coalfields that were about to burst upon the scene.

In April 1973 the remaining four-motor units were renumbered into the 4000-series, usually by simply adding a "4" ahead of their

JIMMY BARLOW

JIM BOYD

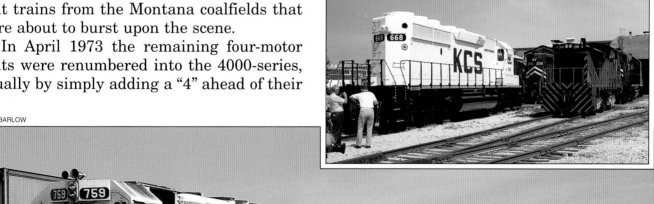

TOM KLINE

three-digit numbers. New motive power over the next decades would be more and more SD40s and their successors, SD40-2s, SD40X's, SD50s and SD60s, as well as new four-motor GP38-2s and GP40-2s. In the 1980s it also turned to the used locomotive market for second-hand SD45s, SD40T-2s, GP40s and even Canadian National comfort cab GP40s.

The white paint prevailed, and the F-unit fleet turned out to be remarkably long-lived. Many units were converted into road slugs, but the veteran covered wagons ran well into the 1980s, with a few of the covered wagon slugs rolling on into the 1990s. In April 1988 the white livery was abandoned in favor of a battleship gray with yellow scare stripes. The first unit repainted gray was SD40-2 652, while the first unit delivered in gray was SD60 714 in December 1989.

DANIEL E. JOHNSON

Mergers and Expansion

When William N. Deramus III died in his Kansas City office on November 15, 1989, his KCS was back on its feet and thriving. While the KCS was under constant threat from the surrounding mega-mergers in the 1990s, it took advantage of the situation to expand and refocus itself. As a byproduct of the UP-Katy merger, the KCS gained much better access to the Dallas gateway, and haulage rights into Houston, Galveston, Omaha and Lincoln. It also purchased the Graysonia, Nashville & Ashdown short line for its chicken-feed business and reached laterally across from Shreveport to Meridian, Miss., by acquiring the Mid-South (the IC's Vicksburg, Shreveport & Pacific) for a short-cut connection with the Southern

THE GRAY ERA began in 1988 and was typified by scenes like SD40-2s and a rebuilt SD45 (above) on the 63rd Street Viaduct at Swope Park on May 7, 2001. The ex-Conrail GP40s (page 125) were renumbered into the 4750s to make room for SD60s; the new 759 (right) was at Meridian, Miss., on March 23, 2002, on trackage acquired with the MidSouth.

On January 15, 2000, GP40 4766, SD40-3 (rebuilt SD45) 619 and SD40X 703 (opposite inset) were crossing the IC/VS&P bridge into Vicksburg on the Shreveport-Meridian route. The KCS got 50 General Electric AC4400CW's in 1999, and ol' Bill Deramus would have loved the sight of 26,400 h.p. on one freight (opposite top) at Hodgens, Okla., on September 28, 2000.

Railway main line, bypassing the congestion of New Orleans. And in 1995 the Louisiana & Arkansas was finally merged into the KCS.

When the National Railways of Mexico was removed form government control and privatized, the KCS got a 50-year operating contract for the Ferrocarril de Noreste from Nuevo Laredo and Matamoros to Mexico City and Vera Cruz. The KCS purchased 49% interest in the Texas-Mexican Railway and some trackage rights over the UP/SP to link the Mexican lines with the KCS at Beaumont. Out of Kansas City, it acquired the Gateway Western (the old GM&O) to St. Louis and Springfield, Ill., and trackage rights into Chicago. This new "NAFTA Railway" (named for the North American Free Trade Agreement) gave the KCS a huge and growing system from Chicago to the heart of Mexico.

Much of this expansion had been made possible by negotiations and concessions from the UP/Katy/SP and BNSF mergers. One of the most interesting byproducts of the BNSF merger was the "spin-off" of the Santa Fe's President Mike Haverty, who took over as head of the KCS in 1995. An admitted railfan, Haverty had brought back the Santa Fe

"Warbonnet" livery for its Super Fleet freight units and had aggressively modernized and promoted traffic on the Santa Fe. His dynamic personality focused international attention on the KCS and gave it a new credibility with both the government and the industry.

In 1998 the KCS even became the first U.S. transcontinental when it was granted a 25-year operating concession for the Panama Railroad, reaching 47 miles from Atlantic to Pacific. In this era of huge "Post-PanaMax" container ships that are too big to fit through the canal, the KCS rebuilt the Panama Railroad to handle double-stack container

MIKE ABALOS

THE SPIRIT AND IMAGE of the "Streamlines Hospitality" era lives on in the 21st Century with F7 73D (above) on display at the Decatur, Ark., depot, where SD60 740 was heading up No.91 with SWEPCO loads on September 11, 1994. Mike Haverty's *New Southern Belle* business train was on a KCS/BNSF special (below) at Ponder, Texas, in August 1999. The ex-CN/VIA F9s and a BNSF coal train were at Knoche Yard in Kansas City (bottom) in July 1999.

trains from coast to coast powered by F40PH's in the classic yellow Southern Belle livery!

And back home, in 1995 Mike Haverty had purchased an A-B-A-A set of ex-Canadian National/VIA Rail Canada HEP-equipped F9s and assembled the "New Southern Belle" business train with the units and cars in the black-with-red-and-yellow passenger car livery.

The KCS entered the 21st Century the same way it had entered the 20th Century, a renegade under the visionary leadership of a dominant personality seeking new horizons. And the new KCS has not forgotten its proud heritage in the process. 🔲

RICH WALLACE

CARL GRAVES